COGNITIVE BEHAVIORAL THERAPY

INTRODUCTION 4

CHAPTER ONE 6

Cognitive Behavioral Therapy 6

CHAPTER TWO22

The History of CBT 22

CHAPTER THREE 32

Basis and Benefits of CBT 32

CHAPTER FOUR 43

Major Cognitive Behavioral Therapies 43

CHAPTER FIVE 86

The Effectiveness of Cognitive Behavioral Therapy 86

CHAPTER SIX 133

Anger Management 133

CHAPTER SEVEN 175

Mindfulness Based Cognitive Behavioral Therapy 176

CHAPTER EIGHT 199

CBT for Anxiety Disorder 200

CHAPTER NINE212

CBT and Psychotherapy Integration.............................212

CHAPTER TEN 238

Overcoming Panic Attacks with CBT.............................238

CONCLUSION 244

INTRODUCTION

CBT tends to deal with the 'here and now'-how you are now affecting your current thoughts and behaviours. It recognizes that events in your past have shaped the way you currently think and behave, particularly in childhood learning thought patterns and behaviors. CBT does not, however, dwell on the past, but aims at finding solutions to change your current thoughts and behaviors so you can function better in the future.

The therapy is based on the simple idea that the way we think directly affects our behaviour, so also our behavior and reaction to situations or events will be irrational when we have irrational or distorted thoughts and perceptions. During CBT sessions, the psychiatrist splits up issues into small pieces, which can be addressed one at a time very quickly. The starting point is a specific situation or event; then the immediate, flawed thoughts of the person on that situation are examined. These mistaken thoughts, often negative, lead the person to have certain emotions and physical feelings, which in turn prompts them to react and act in a negative, unhelpful manner. A trained CBT therapist aims to change the thinking patterns of the patient by demonstrating how much more helpful, rational and positive are their emotions and resulting behaviors when their initial thoughts are correct, realistic and rational.

Clinical trials suggest that CBT has been successful in tackling different emotional issues. Research studies have shown, for example, that a course of CBT is just as effective in treating depression and some anxiety disorders as medication. It is also possible that the effects of CBT will continue to protect the client against further illness in the longer term. People who finish medication may be at higher risk of relapse compared with CBT clients who have learned principles and strategies to sustain their recovery, so problems such as depression or anxiety are less likely to recur in the future, for example. There is also good evidence of research showing that CBT can help improve the symptoms of some physical conditions such as rheumatoid arthritis.

You will learn the nitty-gritty of CBT in this book, and how to best use it. Let's kick off.

CHAPTER ONE

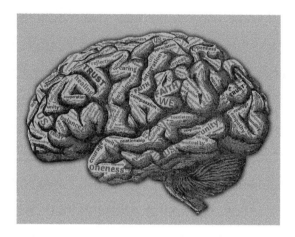

Cognitive Behavioral Therapy

Cognitive behavioral therapy is a type of therapy used to treat specific psychiatric and anxiety problems in a therapeutic manner. Cognitive Behaviour Therapy or CBT has been used consistently since the 1980s to help individuals with psychiatric disorders and to support them with living healthy and fully functional lives.

Cognitive behavioral therapy is just as the name implies, a form of therapy that is used to treat cognitive areas of the well-being of an individual, and to change those cognitive areas in a way that ultimately changes the behavior of an individual.

The foundation of this treatment is that the core feelings or patterns of thought, or cognitions, are the root of unstable or disruptive behavior. By modifying one's cognitions it is expected that the actions of an person will also be changed by CBT.

CBT indicates that when a person encounters skewed feelings that influence their behavior, it induces psychological damage or anxiety. For example, if an adult has an inherent anxiety or believes that squirrels will fall from trees on them, they will avoid trees or walk around trees as they feel this will increase the possibility of a squirrel landing on top of them. CBT will help this individual by training them to rid themselves of this fear of falling squirrels, hoping that this will ultimately change their behaviour, so that one can now walk near trees successfully without this fear or thought process.

CBT works to help individuals identify what the thought processes are that create fears that interfere with their everyday lives. It also works to make an individual aware of the behaviors that result from those faulty processes of thought. CBT 's ultimate task is to help an individual understand how the three elements of thoughts, behaviour, and emotions relate to each other and how these three elements are influenced by external forces or earlier events in life.

Cognitive behavioral therapy (CBT) is an action-oriented, problem-solving therapy that has been found to be highly effective in treating anxiety and depressive disorders. This treatment is uniquely built to treat various patient issues. CBT uses the "here and now" approach, highlighting current life factors that sustain the problem, though past experiences that are directly relevant to the distress of the client are welcomed into the discussion.Cognitive-behavioral therapists help clients realize that while biological and environmental factors that lead to issues, clients produce their own psychological disruptions to a large degree and have the potential to alter these disruptions dramatically. Therapists play an important role in correcting their clients' impaired thoughts, feelings, and attitudes by directing them toward objective expectations and intentions and helping them develop alternate courses of action.

Cognitive counseling lets people realize that skewed cognitive habits are having disturbing mental and behavioural effects. Teaching clients to day-to-day self-monitor their emotions and perceptions by using a routine diary lets them unravel fundamental values and their commitment to current feelings and behaviours. Clients learn to detect and dispute their irrational beliefs during cognitive treatment by discriminating against them from their rational alternatives. Over time, this heightened awareness will lead them to actively challenge their dysfunctional thoughts by using cognitive, emotional , and behavioral change methods.

Behavioral therapy helps clients detect behavioral patterns that are functionally related to the complaint being presented. A behavioral treatment plan is carefully tailored to meet the needs of each individual, and depends on the particular problem at hand. In the presence of phobias or feared situations, techniques such as relaxation training and systematic desensitization are often employed to help clients gradually increase their comfort level. Additionally, modeling, behavior rehearsal, and planned exposures are some of the many tools that help individuals more effectively manage their anxieties.

Cognitive behavioral therapy is one of many forms of psychotherapy that focuses on the emotions or thoughts that could, in some way, cause distress to a person. This form of psychotherapy is often used to help people suffering from anxiety types, depression, or even mood disordered individuals. To do that, the online therapist should aim to work on transforming negative feelings into constructive ones in a patient who may be suffering from depression. If anyone has a phobia, the online psychologist may encourage the patient to picture themselves in a situation that will help them begin to confront their anxiety. If a person has mood disorders, the therapist will be able to find ways to encourage change in the way the patient views things and how they think about different situations. These are some vague examples, but it will hopefully convey the principal idea. To put it simply, cognitive behavioral therapy is where, depending on the patient's trouble, the professional will use different techniques to change the patient's thoughts and/or behavior to more positive, so that the patient can function properly in society without their anxiety, disorder or depression holding them back.

Although it is implied that the only way to get the most out of it is to go to a psychiatrist for this sort of treatment, there are also private counselling people may have to spare themselves the hassle of going out and visiting a doctor in person. It encourages them to take the healing steps from the safety of their home. This could be classified almost as a type of online therapy which can be quite effective in many other cases. Through webcam therapy, personal interaction with the online therapist can often help the patient focus more and possibly work a little faster through the steps than if the patient had stayed home to do so.

How effective is behavioral cognitive therapy? As a result of research done to compare the efficacy of antidepressants and this type of psychotherapy, it has been said by many that cognitive behavioral therapy is just as effective as antidepressants. Research has shown that patients receiving cognitive behavioral therapy have shown the same amount of improvement for their condition as patients receiving medication. A positive point for non-medicinal therapy seemed to show that patients taking cognitive therapy were less likely to relapse into their former condition. So, it seems that cognitive behavioral therapy is probably the better of both options because it has a higher chance of success than the medication that seems to be more of a temporary fix.

Cognitive behavioral therapy or CBT is a combination of two effective therapies. Cognitive therapy applies to the process of thinking and the belief system, whereas behavioral therapy applies to the actions of people. The CBT structure was formed during the 1960s and is used in individual and group therapy settings. Several influential doctors established and perfected it, faced ample scrutiny from the mental health world, and stood the test of time and cynicism.

While more traditional therapies may take years to help a disorder-stricken person, cognitive behavioral therapy is streamlined and it takes as little as seventeen (16) sessions to see positive results. CBT is primarily customer-oriented and created to focus on and tackle a client's problems.

In anxiety disorders and phobia disorders as well as schizophrenia, cognitive behavioral therapy has been shown to be highly successful since the scope is broad and deals with different forms of conditions and mental illnesses. It deals mainly with the here and now, which aims to produce the most successful outcomes.

CBT's strategy is to find out the bull by the horns and deal with things head-on. It helps to reverse processes of negative thinking and to transform behaviors through changing processes of thinking. It is found to be most effective once a client finds for him or herself the best thinking processes and exercises and puts them into daily life.

For instance, cognitive behavioral therapists may employ techniques like:

• How to calm yourself down,

• Curbing negative and destructive thinking using positive affirmations or reinforcements;

• Pay particular attention to the sounds that you listen to and sounds that motivate a person to do other things;

• With a emphasis on unique motives.

The behavioral counseling starts after cognitive patterns are established and treated. It involves applying cognitive techniques to situations in everyday life and in real life. It often involves customer "homework" assignments where the customer visualizes real situations and applies learned techniques to conquer whatever causes problems. Other "homework" might include several times daily practice of positive cognitive techniques. A new strategy is learned until the mind moves from the negative to the positive, and the process proceeds until negative thoughts and actions are gone.

What Constitutes CBT?

Cognitive behavioral therapy is a psychotherapeutic approach aimed at teaching a person new skills on how to solve problems relating to dysfunctional emotions, behaviors and cognitions through a goal-oriented, systematic approach. In many ways, this title is used for differentiating behavioral therapy, cognitive therapy, and therapy based on both behavioral and cognitive therapies. There is scientific evidence that cognitive behavioral therapy is very effective in addressing various problems like temperament, fear, mood, drinking, misuse of drugs, and psychiatric disorders. Treatment is often manualized, as specific psychological orders are treated with specific brief, direct, and time-limited treatments that are driven by techniques.

Cognitive behavioral therapy can be used in groups as well as with individuals. The techniques are also frequently adapted for self-help sessions. Whether he / she is more cognitive oriented, more behavioral oriented, or a combination of both, depends on the individual clinician or researcher, as all three methods are used today. Cognitive behavioral therapy was born out of a combination of cognitive and behavioral therapy. These two treatments had several similarities but find common ground to concentrate on the "here and now" and pain relief.

Evaluating cognitive behavioral therapy has led many to believe that psychodynamic treatments and other methods are more effective than this. The UK promotes the use of computational

Behavioral therapy over other methods for many mental health problems, including post-traumatic stress disorder, obsessive-compulsive disorder, bulimia nervosa, clinical depression, and chronic fatigue syndrome/myalgic encephalomyelitis of the neurological condition. The precursors of cognitive behavioral therapy are rooted in different ancient philosophical traditions, notably Stoicism. The modern roots of CBT can be traced back to the development of behavioral therapy in the 1920s, cognitive therapy development in the 1960s, and subsequent merging of the two therapies. In 1924, Mary Cover Jones published the first psychological approaches to behaviour, whose work deals with the unlearning of fears in adolescents. The early approaches to treatment performed well on many of the neurotic conditions but not so well for depression. The "cognitive revolution" also caused behavioral therapy to lose popularity, which eventually led to the founding of cognitive therapy by Aaron T. Beck in the 1960's. Arnold A. Lazarus developed the first form of cognitive behavioral therapy during the time period from the late 1950s through the 1970s. Cognitive and behavioural treatments were merged during the 1980s and 1990s by research conducted by David M. Clark in the UK and David H. Barlow in the United States. The following systems include cognitive behavioral therapy: cognitive therapy, rational emotional behavior therapy and multimodal therapy. One of the biggest challenges is to define exactly what a cognitive-behavioral treatment is. The specific therapeutic techniques vary among different CBT approaches depending on what kind of problem issues are being addressed, but the techniques usually center around the following:

• Maintaining a diary of significant events and related feelings , thoughts and behaviours.

• Questioning and testing possibly unrealistic and unhelpful cognitions, evaluations, assumptions and beliefs.

• Gradually confronting activities which might have been avoided.

• Try out new ways to behave and react.

In addition, techniques of distraction, mindfulness, and relaxation are also commonly used in cognitive behavioral therapy. Medications that stabilize the mood are also often combined with therapies to treat conditions such as bipolar disorder. The NICE guidelines within the British NHS recognize the application of cognitive behavioral therapy in combination with medication and therapy in treating schizophrenia. Cognitive behavioral therapy usually takes patients time to implement it effectively into their lives. For them, it usually takes concentrated effort to replace a cognitive-affective-behavioral dysfunctional process or habit with a more reasonable and adaptive one, even when they recognize when and where their mental processes go wrong. In many different situations, cognitive behavioral therapy is applied including the following conditions:

• Symptoms of anxiety (obsessive-compulsive disorder, social phobia or social anxiety, general anxiety disorder)

• Mood disorders (clinical depression, psychiatric symptoms, major depressive disorder)

• Insomnia (including being more effective than the Zopiclone medication)

• Extreme psychiatric illnesses (schizophrenia, severe depression, bipolar disorder)

• Children and youth (major signs of depression, anxiety disorders, trauma and post-traumatic stress disorder);

• Stuttering (to help them conquer fear, action evasion and poor thoughts about themselves).

There are a number of treatment approaches within the CBT scope, as defined earlier. These approaches share the theoretical perspective that assumes the occurrence of internal covert processes called "thinking" or "cognition," and cognitive events mediate change of behavior. Indeed, many cognitive-behavioral researchers say specifically that cognition is not only capable of modifying behavior according to the mediational theory, but it must modify actions so that behavioral adjustment can be seen as an indirect measure of cognitive adjustment. Around the same time, these methods suggest that improvements in behaviour do not need to require complex cognitive processes. The treatments can have very little to do with cognitive tests and evaluations of other types of treatment, but they are highly based on individual behavior and improvement of behaviour. CBT 's individual outcomes can inevitably differ from customer to customer, but in general, awareness and behavior are the two key indicators used for improvement. Emotional and physiological changes are also used to a lesser extent as indicators of change in CBT, particularly where emotional or physiological disturbance is a major aspect of the presenting therapy problem (e.g., anxiety disorders, psycho-physiological disorders). One of the trends in the development of the CBTs has been a growing interest in how cognitive mediation affects behavioral, emotional, and physiological processes and how, in practice, these different systems can strengthen one another.

Three major CBT classes have been recognized, as each has a slightly different kind of goals for change. Such courses are strategies for communication skills, problem-solving strategies, and techniques for executive rehabilitation. Since a later section of this chapter details the specific therapies that fall within those CBT categories, this topic is not discussed here. However, what's crucial to note is that the various treatment groups are geared towards different degrees of emotional and behavioral improvement. Coping skills therapies, for example, are primarily used for problems external to the client. In this case, therapy focuses on identifying and altering the ways in which the individual can exacerbate the influence of negative events (e.g. engaging in anxiety-provoking thoughts and images; using avoidance) or using strategies to reduce the impact of negative events (e.g. learning relaxation skills). Thus, the primary success markers within this form of therapy involve behavioral signs of improved coping skills, and concomitant reductions in the consequences of negative events (e.g., less demonstrated anxiety). Cognitive restructuring techniques, by contrast, are more used when the disturbance is created from within the person himself or herself. Such approaches focus on long-term beliefs and situation-specific automatic thinking that gives rise to negative results.

While CBT targets both cognition and behavior as primary area of change, certain types of desired change clearly fall outside of CBT realm. For example, a therapist who adopts a classic conditioning approach to treating self-destructive behavior in an autistic child does not employ a cognitive-behavioral framework; instead, such an approach could be called "behavioral analysis" or "applied behavioral therapy." Indeed, any therapeutic regimen that adopts a stimulus-response model is not a CBT. The term "cognitive-behavioral" should not be used in situations where cognitive therapy can be observed, and where cognitive intervention is an essential part of the recovery program.

Just as purely behavioural treatments are not cognitive — behavioural, they are not exclusively cognitive-behavioral treatments either. For e.g., a therapy approach that indicates memories of a long-held painful experience is not a CBT that induces present mental distress and instead addresses those memories for improvement. It should be noted that this example carries the provision that there is no possible association between the current disorder and past trauma. In a case where a past trauma has occurred and a recent event is highly similar to that in the past, and the client experiences distress as a function of both the past trauma and the current event, cognitive mediation is much more likely, and the therapy may be cognitive-behavioral in nature. CBTs do exist for trauma and its consequences, of course.

Therapies that base their theories on the expression of excessive emotions, as can be seen in cathartic therapy models, are not cognitive-behavioral. Thus, while these therapies may suggest that the emotions are derived from extreme or negative cognitive mediation processes, the lack of a clear mediation model of change puts them outside the CBT field.

The Characteristics of CBT

Cognitive-behavioral therapy is a form of psychotherapy intended to cure people with emotional disorders by focusing on individual behavioral patterns and thinking processes. It is a common term which includes various approaches such as logical emotional therapy, cognitive therapy, dialectical behavioral therapy, ADHD therapy etc. Cognitive behavioral therapy (CBT) has essentially the following features:1. Based on the cognitive model of emotion-related responses: CBT is based on changing people's thoughts and feelings internally rather than depending on outer surroundings, such as people , events or circumstances. That helps the individual to act and feel better even if the situation around him doesn't change.

2. It's fast: Cognitive-behavioral therapy is one of the fastest forms of therapy intended to treat psychological disorders. The systematic treatment finishes when both the client and the therapist are pleased with the demonstrated progress, and the client acquires abilities to cope with similar concerns in the future.

3. Developing a good therapeutic relationship with a focused approach: For proper treatment, a positive relationship between the therapist and the client is required. Therapists who follow CBT approach concentrate on equipping their client with self-counseling skills and thus the client learns to be independent. This can only happen when the patient is at ease with his/her therapist.

4. The efforts are collaborative: CBT therapists strive to learn more about their client's feelings and thoughts. They try to help them attain their life-long goals. A therapist's role is to listen, learn and teach at the same time, while the client 's role is to express his / her concerns, fears frankly and show a willingness to absorb what he / she learns from the therapist.

5. CBT is a standardized and checklist approach to treatment: A clear agenda is set for each CBT session. The client's instructional methods are matched with their particular expectations.

6. CBT theory is based on induction model: The inductive method is adopted to encourage people to distinguish myths and hypotheses from reality and the practicalities of life. This helps the person accept the real and discard the unreal negative thoughts that pull him down.

7. Client homework: Clients are asked to apply the skills and techniques they are taught during the therapy sessions. The client can not overcome his/her problem without practising them. Homework therefore becomes an unavoidable part of Cognitive Behavioral Therapy.

CHAPTER TWO

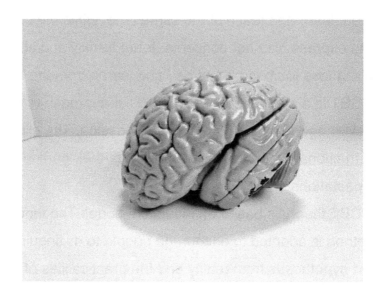

The History of CBT

Cognitive behavioural therapy is a technique psychotherapists use to manipulate the attitudes and feelings of a individual. The key to the approach is what must be systematic in its procedure. It was successfully used to treat a variety of disorders including eating disorders, abuse of substances, anxiety and personality disorders. It can be used in individual or group therapy sessions and the approach to self-help therapy can also be geared to.

Cognitive behavioural therapy is a mixture of cognitive therapy and conventional behavioral therapy. They are combined into a treatment that focuses on eliminating the symptoms. The treatment 's efficacy can be clearly judged on the basis of its results. The more that is used, the more recommended it has become. It is now used as the number one post-traumatic stress disorder treatment technique, obsessive compulsive disorder, depression and bulimia.

The earliest use of cognitive behavioural therapy occurred in 1960-1970. It has been a gradual process of merging the techniques of behavioral therapy and cognitive therapy. Behavioral therapy has been available since the 1920s but it was not until the 1960s that cognitive therapy was adopted. The benefits of combining it with behavioral therapy techniques had been realized almost immediately. Ivan Pavlov was among the most famous of the pioneers of behavioral research with his dogs who salivated at the dinner bell ringing. Other field leaders included Clark Hull and John Watson. Instead of focusing on analysis of the problem such as Freud and the psychoanalysts, cognitive behavioral therapy focused on eliminating the symptoms. The theory is, you solved the problem if you remove the signs. This more direct approach has been seen as being more effective in getting to the problem at hand and helping patients make faster progress. Behavioral approaches cope more with more conventional conditions than a more conventional punitive procedure. The more evident and straightforward the signs were, the better it was for them to be identified and for them to be eliminated. Behavioral therapy, initially with more ambiguous problems such as depression, was not as successful. Cognitive therapy techniques have served this realm better.

The two therapy techniques were used side by side, in many academic settings, to compare and contrast the results. It wasn't long before the advantages of integrating the two strategies were apparent as a way to take advantage of each 's strengths. David Barlow 's work on overcoming panic disorder offered the first clear indication of the combination strategy 's effectiveness.

In a concise term, cognitive behavioral therapy is hard to describe, as it encompasses such a broad variety of subjects and strategies. It is really a paragliding definition for individual treatments that are specifically tailored to a particular patient 's problems. So the problem dictates the treatment specifics, but some common themes and techniques do exist. These include keeping the patient a diary of important events and recording their feelings and behaviors associated with each event. This tool is then used as a basis for analyzing and testing the patient's ability to assess the situation and develop a suitable emotional response. It identifies negative emotions and behaviors, as well as the assessments and beliefs that lead to them. Then an effort is made to counter those beliefs and assessments to show that the resulting behaviors are wrong.

Bad attitudes are removed, and a healthier way for the individual to perceive and react to the situation is learned.

Part of the treatment also involves showing the patient how to redirect or shift their attention from the disturbing, or a condition that creates unpleasant behavior. Instead of the negative stimulus, they learn to focus on something else, eliminating the negative behavior that this would lead to. Essentially the problem gets nipped in the bud. Mood stabilizing medications are often prescribed to use in conjunction with these techniques for serious psychological disorders such as bipolar disorder or schizophrenia. The drugs give the patient ample soothing influence to enable them to analyze the condition and make a healthier decision, while before they may not pause for critical thought.

Two historic strands serve as historical foundations for the CBTs. The dominant strand relates to behavioral therapies, often perceived as the primary precursor of CBTs. CBTs also evolved to a lesser extent from psycho-dynamic therapy models. Behavioral therapy was an innovation from the radical approach to human problems of conduct. It built on the classical and operational behavioral conditioning concepts, and developed a series of behavioral change-focused approaches. However, a shift that began to occur in behavioral therapy in the 1960s and 1970s made it possible to develop cognitive-behavior theory, and more broadly, a logical necessity for CBT. First, although the behavioral perspective had been a dominant force for some time, by the late 1960s it became apparent that a non-mediation approach was not sufficiently expansive to account for all human behaviour. Bandura's (1965, 1971) accounts of vicarious learning defied traditional explanation of behaviour, as did Mischel, Ebbesen, and Zeiss's (1972) work on delay of gratification. Similarly, children were learning grammatical rules well outside the ability of most parents and educators to strengthen discriminatively, and serious attacks were being made on behavioral models of language learning. The effort to extend these models to include "covert" habits was yet another example of frustration with behavioral models. Although this approach met with some limited optimism, it was apparent from behavioral quarters criticisms that such extensions were not consistent with the behavioral emphasis on overt phenomena.

A second factor facilitating CBT 's development was that the very nature of certain issues, such as obsessional thinking, made non-cognitive interventions irrelevant. Behavioral therapy as was appropriate was applied to disorders primarily demarcated by their behavioral correlates. Behavioral therapists also targeted the behavioral symptoms for change in multifaceted disorders. This behavioral focus provided a significant increase in therapeutic potential over past efforts but was not entirely satisfactory to therapists who recognized that all problems, or major components of problems, were going untreated. Developing cognitive behavioural therapy strategies helped fill a void in the clinical methods of the clinician.

Third, the psychological landscape in general was evolving, and cognitivism, or what was termed the "cognitive movement," was a big part of the transition. Within the context of experimental psychology a variety of mediational principles were developed, researched and created. These models, perhaps the most influential of which was the cognition model of information processing, were explicitly mediational and received substantial support from cognition labs. One of the natural developments was the extension to clinical constructs of information — processing models.

In the 1960s and 1970s a number of researchers carried out basic research into the cognitive mediation of clinically relevant constructs, even beyond the development of general cognitive models. For example, Lazarus and associates have documented that anxiety during this time period involves cognitive mediation in a number of studies. Taken together, behavioral theorists were challenged by the two research areas of general cognitive psychology and what might be called "applied cognitive psychology" to account for the accumulating data. Essentially, the challenge was a need for behavioral models to redefine their boundaries and integrate cognitive processes in the behavioral dynamics models. Perhaps one of the earliest signs of this attempt to incorporate can be seen in the literature on self-regulation and self-control developed in the early 1970s. All these different attempts to delineate self-control perspectives on behavioral modification shared the idea that the individual has some capacity to monitor his or her behavior, set behavioral goals generated internally, and orchestrate environmental and personal variables in order to achieve some form of regulation in inter-est behaviour. Several cognitive mechanisms needed to be proposed to establish such self-control models, including efforts to describe self-control techniques primarily in terms of the internal "cybernetic" working components.

The second historical thread that conspired to contribute to the cognitive — behavioral field was that of psycho-dynamic theory and counseling in addition to behaviorism. Just as there was growing dissatisfaction with strict behaviorality, the strongest alternative perspective, the psycho-dynamic model of personality and therapy, continued to be rejected. Early research in the CBT field included remarks summarily denying psychoanalytic reliance on unconscious mechanisms, evaluating historical content, and the need for long-term treatment focused on the production of understanding in the transference – counter-transfer relationship. However, it remains an interesting fact that the work of Aaron Beck and

Albert Ellis, the two leading figures in the field whose early training was psycho-dynamic in nature, both later develop variants of CBT that emphasized cognitive restructuring, and the need for more trait-like and persistent beliefs or schemes for analysis and potential change.

Beyond the methodological contradictions with some of the core tenets of psycho-dynamic theories, the outcomes research reviews indicated that the success of traditional psychotherapy was not especially noteworthy. Maybe the boldest evaluative statement on the proven success of psycho-dynamic treatments came from Rachman and Wilson (1980), who said that "there is currently little appropriate evidence to support the argument that psychoanalysis is an successful therapy." Most of the themes found in the early cognitive-behavioral therapists whose research originated from psycho-dynamic contexts was an emphasis on short-term pain reduction and dilemma solving.

As is valid for every social movement, the creation and recognition of a variety of thinkers and practitioners who described themselves as joining this movement was a crucial feature of the early growth of the CBTs. Beck (1967, 1970), Cautela (1967, 1969), Ellis (1962, 1970), Mahoney (1974), Mahoney and Thoresen (1974), and Meichenbaum (1973, 1977) were some of the people who explicitly initiated this process. Clearly, having some primary advocates of a cognitive-behavioral viewpoint had the effect of generating a zeitgeist that drew many people's interest in the area. Furthermore, the creation of a journal specifically tailored to the emerging cognitive — behavioral field contributed to this trend. Thus, the founding of Cognitive Therapy and Science in 1977, with Michael Mahoney as its inaugural editor, created a platform "to promote and convey study and theory on the role of cognitive processes in human evolution and development" (from the journal's cover). The existence of a regular cognitive-behavior theory and modification publication has enabled researchers and therapists to present to a wide audience provocative ideas and research findings.

A final critical recent aspect that has led to a growing interest in the cognitive-behavioural context has been the publication of empirical findings that have shown cognitive-behavioral therapy results to be as or more beneficial than purely behavioral interventions. In a critical review of cognitive-behavioral modification, Ledgewidge (1978) reviewed 13 studies that contrasted cognitive-behavioral versus behavioral therapies and found no evidence of superiority for either, although he noted that the studies he reviewed were based on analogous populations, and clinical trials were necessary for a more summative judgment. The highly negative analysis by Ledgewidge provoked a response that largely ignored his critiques as "premature" (Mahoney & Kazdin, 1979). After this early debate over the effectiveness of CBTs, a number of studies have clearly shown that CBTs have a therapeutic impact. The CBTs are indeed notable for their presence in the list of empirically supported therapies. However, it is important to note that clinical success meta-analysis challenges the degree to which cognitive behavioral interventions are equivalent to purely behavioral therapies. As the database is further enlarged it will be possible to make more definitive statements about the effectiveness of these types of therapy. What we think will come from continuing work is concrete findings not only about the general efficacy of CBTs but also clear claims about the relative effectiveness of various forms of CBTs for particular types of clinical problems.

From this review it becomes apparent that there have been and continue to exist a number of compelling reasons for the development of cognitive — behavioral dysfunction and therapy models. These reasons include dissatisfaction with previous therapy models, clinical problems highlighting the need for a cognitive-behavioral perspective, research on cognitive aspects of human functioning, the contemporary phenomenon that has led to an identified group of cognitive-behavioral theorists and therapists, and the growing body of research that supports the clinical effectiveness With this general trend in mind, we now give more in-depth summaries of the historical developments behind the large number of specific CBTs that have evolved over the past 40 years or so.

CHAPTER THREE

Basis and Benefits of CBT

Cognitive-behavioral therapy is a form of psychotherapy that stresses the important role that thinking plays in how we feel and what we do.

There is no cognitive-behavioral therapy as a distinct therapeutic technique. The term "cognitive-behavioral therapy (CBT)" for a classification of therapies with similarities is a very general term. Cognitive-behavioral therapy has several approaches, including Rational Emotional Behavior Therapy, Rational Behavior Therapy, Rational Living Therapy, Cognitive Therapy, and Dialectic Behavior Therapy.

Most cognitive-behavioral therapies, however, have the following characteristics:

1. CBT is based on a Cognitive Emotional Response Model. Cognitive-behavioral therapy is based on the idea that our thoughts, like people , situations, and events, cause our feelings and behaviours, not external things. The benefit of this fact is that even if the situation doesn't change, we can change the way we think we feel/act better.

2. CBT is Time-Limited and Briefer.

In terms of the results obtained, cognitive-behavioral therapy is considered among the most rapid. The average number of clients receiving sessions (over all types of CBT problems and approaches) is only 16. Other forms of treatment can take years, such as psychoanalysis. What makes CBT briefer is its highly instructive nature and the fact that it uses assignments from homework. CBT is time-limited in that at the very beginning of the therapy process, we help clients understand that there will be a point when the formal therapy is to end. The termination of formal therapy is a decision of the therapist and the client. CBT is, therefore, not an open-ended, interminable process.

3. For successful counseling a strong marital partnership is important but not the emphasis. Any types in treatment believe that the biggest reason people feel happier in treatment is that the psychiatrist and the client share a good relationship.

Cognitive-behavioral therapists think a good, trusting relationship is important, but that is not enough. CBT therapists believe the clients are changing because they are learning how to think differently and acting on that learning. CBT practitioners also concentrate on developing appropriate self-control skills.

4. CBT is a collaborative effort between patient and therapist. Cognitive-behavioral therapists try to understand about experience what their clients desire (their goals) and then support their clients in meeting those goals. The role of the therapist is to listen, teach, and encourage, whereas the roles of the client are to express concerns, learn, and implement that learning.

5. CBT has stoic philosophy as its basis.

Not all CBT approaches underpin stoicism. Stoicism is emphasized by rational emotional behavior therapy, rational behavior therapy, and rational living treatment. Cognitive Therapy with Beck is not based on stoicism. Cognitive-behavioral therapy doesn't say how people should feel. Most people seeking therapy, however, don't want to feel the way they felt. The approaches that stress stoicism demonstrate the advantages of staying relaxed when faced with unexpected circumstances, at worst. They also underline the fact that we are having our unwanted situations whether we are upset about them or not. If we're upset about our problems, we 're having two problems — the problem, and our anger over it.

Most people want the fewest possible number of problems. So when we learn to accept a personal problem more calmly, we not only feel better but usually put ourselves in a better position to use our intelligence, knowledge, energy, and resources to solve the problem.

6. CBT employs the Socratic Method.

Cognitive-behavioral therapists are looking to gain a very good understanding of the concerns of their clients. That is why they ask questions frequently. They always inspire their clients to ask themselves questions, such as, "How do I really know those people are laughing at me?" "Will they laugh at someone else?"

7. CBT is organized and directive.

For each session, the cognitive-behavioral therapists have a clear agenda. During each session specific techniques/concepts will be taught. CBT focuses on customer objectives. We don't tell our customers what their goals should be, or tolerate what they "should." We are a guideline in the sense that we are explaining to our customers how to act and respond in ways to achieve what they want. CBT therapists, therefore, don't tell their clients what to do — rather, they teach their clients how to do it.

8. The CBT is based upon a model of education.

CBT is based on the assumption that most emotional and behavioral reactions are learnt. The goal of the therapy is, therefore to help clients unlearn their unwanted reactions and learn a new way to react. So CBT has nothing to do with just talking. People can talk to anyone, "just talk." CBT 's educational accent has an added benefit — it leads to long-term results. When people understand how they do well, and why they do well, they know what to do to keep doing well.

9. The Inductive Method relies on CBT theory and techniques.

The central feature of critical reasoning is that it is fact-based. We sometimes get angry over issues when, in reality, the situation is not the way we think it is. If we knew that, we wouldn't be wasting our time getting angry. The inductive method, therefore, encourages us to look at our thoughts as hypotheses or guesses which can be questioned and tested. If we find our hypotheses wrong (because we have new information), then we can change our thinking to be in line with the actual situation.

10. Homework is a staple of CBT.

If you spent only one hour per week studying them when you tried to learn your multiplication tables, you might still wonder what 5 x 5 equals. You've most definitely spent a lot of time practicing the multiplication tables at home, even with flashcards. The same is true of psychotherapy. Goal achievement (if attained) could take a very long time if all a person had to think only about the techniques and subjects taught was one hour a week. That is why CBT therapists are assigning read assignments and encouraging their clients to practice the learned techniques.

The Benefits of CBT

As the name implies, cognitive behavioural therapy (CBT) is a combination of two psychological approaches: cognitive and behavioral therapy. Although the two approaches are totally different from each other, they have been combined because psychologists have this common belief that a thought or cognition mainly pushes for or causes any action.

So for them, it follows that when a person starts to change their way of thinking about themselves, their behavior usually follows through. And this thought-behavioral relationship is found to be ideal in helping mood disorder patients.

As such, the use of cognitive behavioral therapy to treat clinical depression is extensive. Why do you ask for this method among others? Well that is obviously because the advantages of CBT are as follows:

2. They 're less intrusive. For example, if you have a moderate case of depression, you don't even need to take treatment. Hypnosis and a couple of sessions with a support group or a psychologist might even do that for you.

2. Unlike medicine, over long stretches of time, this is not something you get to hold or even live with. You should get on with your life because you are already "set," and continue to do the things you enjoy. Plus, if there is a relapse danger, you will still get urgent support back to the care.

3. Perhaps it's one approach which can make a patient feel good. This is mainly due to the fact that these cognitive behavior therapy sessions essentially teach a person with a mood disorder to remove all of the negativity in their system and expel any stimuli that will not help them in their life.

4. Cognitive behavioural therapy actually succeeds. Based on current statistics, the use of this approach (alone or in combination with other methods) has been shown to increase a patient's likelihood of getting better by at least 75 percent. More than that, it has been said that people who have been subjected to CBT experience long term results.

Cognitive therapy is a type of psychological treatment operated in the area of multiple human emotions, influenced by thoughts, beliefs and attitudes. Aaron Beck, M.D was the pioneer in introducing cognitive therapy as a major treatment for depression, panic, anger control, and other psychological related issues.

Cognitive therapy is used primarily in different stages of depression. Depression is caused for many causes. Biological transition, negative obstinacy, catastrophic accidents may cause depression. Yet in all depression related situations one thing is typical & it is pointless critical thought. Depressed people can think to any matter in the most negative way possible. This inclination toward negative thought causes a feeling of fear among them. In that moment of depression, cognitive therapy comes into the picture. Cognitive therapy is a special way of treatment that helps individuals identify the negative ways of thinking and then guide them to rectify their thinking. Ultimately, it helps people who are depressed think positively and logically, which can reduce depression.

It's truly a misconception that only "positive thinking" can reduce depression levels. To reduce depression, thinking with a positive attitude is very important, but more important is to learn to identify the negative thoughts and convert them into positive note. Since it is very clear that suicidal people can not avoid negative thinking, they should be encouraged to learn to recognise their negative thoughts. Cognitive therapy will do so of all treatments most clinically. In addition , cognitive therapy helps depressed people dispute their negative thoughts once they are able to identify them. Cognitive Therapy can work as a marvel for any depressed person with precise and long-lasting practice.

But it should also be remembered that cognitive therapy is not a magic therapy with which a depressed fellow can be transformed into a cheerful guy in a month or so. To get the most benefit out of cognitive therapy, it is really important to master the fundamental skills at the initial level. The much-needed skills in cognitive therapy are self-monitoring of the stream of thoughts, identifying negative thoughts, ideas and attitudes and ultimately thinking in a more realistic way that alters the negative approach. At first, adopting the preliminary Cognitive Therapy sessions becomes very difficult. However, long-lasting practice in simple skills may have more effect on the stressed and provide more relaxation. And, to achieve the greatest benefit, it is also best to learn the fundamental skills of cognitive therapy as much as possible.

In the initial phase of cognitive-behavioral therapy, a therapist may ask the patient to fill in a variety of questions of the self-assessment type. The main reason is to get a glimpse of the patient's symptoms and problems. These questions assess mental factors such as personality, state of mind, depression, anxiety, anger etc. This unusual way of studying a single patient's problems is very useful. The therapist can then begin treatment. One of the greatest advantages of cognitive therapy is tailoring the treatment method.

The 3 Phases of CBT

In a nutshell, cognitive behavioral therapy is an anxiety disorder that must be addressed through therapy, focusing on its three main areas. Cognitive; which is the process of thinking and of believing. Next is behavioral; what do we do, and how do we do it. Last is Emotional; it is relaxation, harmony, energy, and power techniques.

People have often questioned if this type of therapy would benefit. More recently, clinical evidence has since found that such approaches can be more effective than medications recommended for depression , anxiety and obsessive styles. This is excellent news as drugs have known adverse effects, and CBT really teaches you how to treat the root issues through self-help approaches which, in essence, help people prevent relapses.

Your psychiatrist will help you set concrete expectations in the first step, targets that you like. This is done by taking a hard look at how you see things, and helping you see things differently. Change your ways of thinking, change your way of thinking. You 're going to learn to put a spin on things in a positive way, like if you've always assumed that only negative things are going to come your way, then they might. If you redirect your thinking, instead, you'll learn to expect positive and healthier outcomes.

For eg, your sessions have too many different avenues to dig into; just slow down, make logical thinking even more intuitive and more concentrated and determined. You can also expect to deal with anger, frustration and overall how you handle things.

This is how you tailor all these improvements to suit into your real life scenarios in the next step. You will need a real understanding of these practices, so you can put your newly learned emotional skills and strategies into the challenges of your daily lives. If you are suffering from social anxieties, you will need to feel a little more comfortable before getting in front of a group of people and delivering a speech.

You won't focus on the strength and power in the emotional therapy sessions, this will come naturally over time. You need to work on the relaxing. Your brain needs to de-stress itself and be able to absorb calmness and peace. This will help foster a positive perspective on life, as well as healing and harmony within. There's a process here, allowing the peace and calm to expand slowly, you'll inadvertently let the anxieties, fear and stress escape from nature.

CHAPTER FOUR

Major Cognitive Behavioral Therapies

CBTs represent the convergence of behavioral strategies and cognitive processes, with the objective of achieving cognitive and behavioral change. But even a brief review of the therapeutic procedures subsumed under the CBT heading reveals a variety of principles and practices. Diversification of cognitive-behavioral strategy development and application can be explained in part by the various theoretical orientations of those who developed therapeutic approaches based on this viewpoint. For instance, the authors of rational emotional behavior therapy and cognitive therapy Ellis and Beck came from psychoanalytic backgrounds, respectively. By comparison, Goldfried, Meichenbaum, and Mahoney were initially educated in behaviour modification theory.

Mahoney and Arnkoff (1978) grouped the CBTs into three major divisions: (1) executive development, (2) communication ability therapy and (3) problem-solving therapy. Therapies included under the heading "cognitive restructuring" assume that the consequence of ill-adaptive thoughts is emotional distress. Thus, the aim of these clinical interventions is to examine and challenge ill-adaptive patterns of thought and to establish more adaptive patterns of thought. In comparison, the emphasis of "coping skills therapy" is on building a set of techniques intended to help the person deal with a variety of difficult conditions. The "problem-solving therapies" may be characterized as a combination of cognitive restructuring techniques and training processes for coping skills. Problem-solving therapies emphasize the development of general strategies to address a wide range of personal issues and emphasize the importance of active collaboration between client and therapist in planning the treatment programme. In the following pages, we explain the evolution of the cognitive — behavioral paradigm linked main therapies. This analysis is not intended to be comprehensive and therefore excludes a variety of therapies which have not prompted a large amount of testing or clinical use.

Rational Emotive Behavior Therapy

Many consider rational emotive behavioral therapy (REBT) to be the first example of the cognitive-behavioral approach. Albert Ellis developed the fundamental theory and implementation of REBT almost 50 years ago. After extensive training and experience in psychoanalysis, Ellis started to question the effectiveness and effectiveness of the classical analytical method. He observed that patients tended to remain in therapy for long periods of time, and often resisted psychoanalytic techniques such as free association and dream analysis. In addition, Ellis questioned whether the personal insight assumed by psychoanalytic theory led to therapeutic change led to lasting changes in behaviour: But still, I wasn't satisfied with the results that I got. For, again, in a fairly short time, a large number of patients improved considerably and felt much better after gaining some seemingly crucial insights. But few of them, in the sense of being minimally assaulted with anxiety or hostility, were really cured. And, as before, patient after patient would say to me: "Yes, I see exactly what is bothering me now, and why I'm bothered by it; but I'm bothered yet. What can I do on this now? Discouraged by the limitations of the analytical method, Ellis began experimenting with more active treatment techniques and directives.

He formulated a theory of emotional disturbance and a set of treatment methods through a process of clinical trial and error, which emphasized a practical approach to dealing with life problems. Although advocates of analytic theory considered Ellis' methods heretical, the advent of behavioral therapy in the 1960s and the increasing acceptance of the role of cognitions in understanding human behavior eventually encouraged the acceptance of REBT (formerly called rational emotional therapy [RET]) as a potentially valid alternative to the more traditional models of psychotherapy. At the heart of REBT lies the assumption that human thinking and emotion are interrelated significantly.

According to the ABC model of Ellis, symptoms are the consequences (C) of the irrational belief systems (B) of a person with respect to particular activating experiences or events (A). The therapy goal is to identify the irrational beliefs at the root of emotional disturbance and challenge them. REBT assumed that people have innate and acquired tendencies to think and act irrationally. Thus individuals must constantly monitor and challenge their basic beliefs systems in order to maintain a state of emotional health. Ellis (1970) identified 12 fundamental irrational beliefs taking the general form of unrealistic or absolute expectations.

REBT believes that large shifts in feelings and attitudes will occur by replacing unreasonable, overgeneralized expectations with rational needs , interests, or wishes. Since individuals tend to preserve their irrational patterns of thought forcefully, however, significant and lasting changes require powerful methods of intervention. REBT employs a multidimensional approach that combines methods of perception, feeling, and behaviour.

Nevertheless, the main therapeutic tool remains a "logical - empirical method of scientific questioning, challenging, and debating" designed to help individuals surrender irrational beliefs. In addition to dispute, REBT therapists use a wide variety of techniques, including self-monitoring of thoughts, biblio-therapy, role-playing, modeling, rational emotional imaging, shame-attacking exercises, relaxation methods, operant conditioning, and skills training. REBT's theory and practice are largely identical to when the approach was first introduced. Thus, as outlined in his book Reason and Emotion in Psychotherapy (1962), Ellis' original conceptualization of RET remains a primary reference for this approach. Renaming RET to become REBT did not signify a shift of theory or focus, as much as it represented Ellis' willingness to portray the specific expectations of REBT therapists more accurately. His conceptual focus is one of the main distinctions between REBT and other cognitive behavioral approaches.

The distinctly philosophical outlook of Ellis (1980) is reflected in what he identified as REBT's main objectives: self-interest, social interest, self-direction, self-tolerance and others, flexibility, acceptance of uncertainty, commitment to vital interests, self-acceptance, scientific thinking, and a non-utopian perspective on life. REBT assumes that there will be minimal emotional disturbance among individuals who adopt this type of rational philosophy. REBT has generated a wide range of literature and is applied to areas as diverse as leadership and business, as well as schools.

Unfortunately, REBT advocates have authored most of the published articles rather than researchers concerned with collecting objective data about their validity and utility (Mahoney, 1979). However, other publications say that REBT is starting to undergo the rigorous scientific analysis which was lacking in the past.

Cognitive Therapy

Aaron Beck, the cognitive therapy producer, had been previously educated in psycho-analysis. Like Ellis, Beck started challenging neurosis psychoanalytic theories, particularly with regard to depression. In 1963, Beck found that depression-related cognitive causes were mostly overlooked in favour of psychoanalytic focus on motivational – affective conceptualizations. However, based on an inquiry into the thematic nature of clinical patients' cognitions, Beck was able to discern clear variations in the ideational nature of specific neurotic conditions, including depression. He has also observed that patients exhibit systemic inconsistencies in their patterns of thought. Consequently, he generated a typology of cognitive distortions to describe those systematic errors that included the now well-known concepts of arbitrary inference, selective abstraction, over-generalization, magnification, and minimization.

A five year research project at the University of Pennsylvania culminated in the Depression: Causes and Treatment published in 1967. Beck described his cognitive model and addiction treatment, and other neuroses, in this volume. A second book, Cognitive Therapy and Emotional Disorders (Beck, 1976), outlined the specific cognitive distortions associated with each of the neuroses in more detail and described the cognitive therapy principles, with special reference to depression. In 1979, Beck co-authored a comprehensive depression treatment manual, which presented cognitive interventions developed over the past decade of clinical work and investigation (Beck, Rush, Shaw, & Emery, 1979). This book, Cognitive Depression Therapy, remains a crucial resource in the field and has served as the manual of care for a large body of outcome studies.

Beck 's model (1970) was extended from the early emphasis on depression to other disorders and difficulties, including anxiety, bipolar disorder, marital problems (Beck, 1988), personality disorders, substance use issues, crisis management, anger (Beck, 1999), and psychosis. The cognitive model has maintained a focus throughout these developments on the way distorted thinking and unrealistic cognitive assessments of events can negatively affect one's feelings and behaviour. Therefore it is assumed that his or her affective state is determined by the way an individual structures reality. In fact, the cognitive paradigm indicates that there is a mutual interaction between mood and cognition, and that one appears to improve the other, leading to a potential worsening of mental and cognitive dysfunction.

"Schemes" are defined as cognitive structures that organize incoming information and process it. Schemes are proposed to represent the organized patterns of thought that are acquired early in the development of an individual and develop with accumulated experiences over the lifetime. Although well-adjusted personality systems allow for rational appraisal of life circumstances, ill-adjusted individuals result in skewed expectations, dysfunctional problem-solving problems, and psychiatric disorders. For example, the schematic processes of depressed individuals can be characterized by a negative cognitive triad in which views of the self (self as a "loser"), the world (the world is harsh and demanding, and leads to helplessness) and the future (the future is bleak and hopeless) are disturbed.

The primary objective of cognitive therapy is to replace the presumed distorted assessments of life events by more realistic and adaptive assessments of the client. Care is based on a collective, psycho-educational approach requiring the creation of unique learning environments for educating clients to:

(1) monitoring automatic thinking;

(2) Recognize the cognitive, affective and behavioral relations;

(3) Check automated thinking for their validity;

(4) Confuse more rational cognitions with warped thoughts; and

(5) Identify and alter the underlying beliefs , assumptions or schemes predisposing individuals to faulty patterns of thought.

Unlike REBT, Beck 's cognitive psychopathology theory and cognitive techniques underwent a substantial degree of empirical scrutiny. Cognitive stress treatment is now considered a viable solution to clinical and physiological treatments. In fact, cognitive therapy has superior efficacy to pharmacotherapy for anxiety disorders. The generalizability of the Beck paradigm and intervention, and the effectiveness of medication in comparison to other psychiatric illnesses, needs more study. Nevertheless, Beck's and his associates' contributions have had a significant impact on both researchers and clinicians, and are likely to continue to stimulate research for many years to come.

Self-Instructional Training

During a period when behavioral therapy flourished, the clinical interests of Donald Meichenbaum developed, and the then-radical ideas of Ellis (1962), Beck (1970), and other advocates of cognitive treatment approaches began to attract the attention of a new generation of clinicians. In this context, Meichenbaum (1969) conducted a doctoral research program exploring the effects of an operant therapy technique on psychiatric schizophrenic patients learned to emit "good speaking." He found that patients who were engaged in random self-instruction to "speak good" were less distracted and demonstrated superior task performance on a number of scales. This observation gave impetus to a research programme, which focused on the role of cognitive factors in behavioral change.

Meichenbaum 's work was strongly influenced by two Soviet psychologists, Luria (1961) and Vygotsky (1962), who researched the verbal, perception and behavioral developmental relations. They suggested that developing voluntary control over one's behavior involves a gradual progression from external regulation to self-regulation by significant others (e.g., parental instructions) as a result of internalizing verbal commands. As a result, the association between verbal self-instruction and actions became Meichenbaum 's key research subject. He proposed that covert behaviors function under the same standards as overt behaviors, thus subjecting covert behaviors to change using the same coping techniques used to alter overt behaviors. Early efforts by Meichenbaum to investigate the feasibility of this concept included the creation of a self-instructional training curriculum (SIT) intended to remedy impulsive children's intervention deficiencies. The Treatment program 's objectives were fourfold:

(1) Train impulsive children to generate and respond appropriately to verbal self-commands;

(2) To improve the persuasion properties of the inner discourse of chil-dren to put their actions under their own verbal control;

(3) Overcoming any shortcomings in perception, development or mediation; and

(4) Encouraging children to appropriately regulate their behaviour.

The specific procedures were conceived to replicate the sequence of development outlined by Luria (1961) and Vygotsky (1962):

(1) A model exercised the task of speaking aloud while a child was observing;

(2) The infant carried out the same task, while the model received verbal instructions;

(3) The child accomplished the task while being instructed aloud;

(4) While whispering instructions the child performed the task; and

(5) The child carried out the task in a covert manner.

The program's self-instructions included:

(1) Questions concerning the essence and demands of the task;

(2) A cognitive rehearsal of the answers to these questions;

(3) Self-guidance instructions when executing the mission, and

(4) Fortifying oneself.

Meichenbaum and Goodman (1971) found that self-educational training significantly improved impulsive children's task performance across a number of care and control group measures.

Encouraged by their initial research results, Meichenbaum and his associates sought to expand and refine SIT. Further investigations were designed to examine SIT's ability to generalize in the treatment of a variety of psychological disorders, including schizophrenia, speech anxiety, test anxiety, and phobias (Mahoney, 1974).

Meichenbaum 's behavioral background is evident in the procedural emphasis SIT places on graduated tasks, cognitive modelling, guided mediation training, and self-reinforcement. SIT provides a basic paradigm of treatment that may be modified to suit the specific needs of a particular clinical population. Clients are generally trained in six global self-instruction skills:

(1) Description of Problems,

(2) An approach to problems,

(3) Focusing attention,

(4) Statements on coping with,

(5) Miscellaneous options, and

(6) Self-reinforcement.

SIT 's versatility is perhaps one of its most attractive qualities and, not necessarily, a large literature has developed on SIT 's utility for a number of psychiatric disorders.

In recent years, the primary use of SIT appears to be in the treatment of youth, mentally handicapped individuals, and in some areas, such as athletics, where specific skill training is required. It does not tend to frequently act as a stand-alone treatment, but SIT is often used to establish and promote a greater sense of self-efficacy and capacity in the form of a wider range of approaches. An interesting side note is that since SIT was developed Meichenbaum's clinical interests have shifted. He developed a constructive, narrative approach to the posttraumatic stress disorder problem (Meichenbaum, 1994), in which more traditional SIT methods are not largely reflected. He also retains an awareness and participation in the research on stress inoculation.

Self-Control Treatments

Within the wide field of CBT, a number of approaches have been created that concentrate on the self and its control in various settings. These approaches used terms such as "self-efficacy," "self-control," and "self-regulation" to emphasize the hypothetical use of these broad interventions in many different contexts (Kanfer, 1970, 1971).

Marvin Goldfried was among the growing number of clinicians in the early 1970s who challenged the appropriateness of learning theory and advocated the incorporation of cognitive processes into human behavior conceptualizations. He supported the shift in emphasis from discrete, situation-specific responses and problem-specific procedures to a focus on coping skills that could be applied across modalities of response, situations, and issues. In 1971, in contrast to Wolpe's (1958) counter-conditioning model, Goldfried proposed that systematic desensitization be conceptualized in terms of a general mediational model. Goldfried viewed "systematic desensitization" as a way to give clients a general willingness to calm themselves. In an attempt to transform desensitization into a more comprehensive training program for the coping skills, four components were emphasized:

(1) Description of the therapeutic rationale for the training of skills;

(2) Use of relaxation as a generalized or multi-purpose strategy for coping;

(3) Implementation of multitheme hierarchies, and

(4) Scenic "relaxation" preparation — triggered anxiety as opposed to the conventional approach of ending the fictional scene at the first sign of subjective pain.

Goldfried's alignment to coping strategies finally contributed to the creation of a strategy dubbed "systematic logical reform." Borrowing from Dollard and Miller's (1950) research on the emergence of relational thought systems, Goldfried and Sobocinski (1975) proposed that early social learning interactions teach us various ways to mark circumstances. They argued that emotional reactions could be understood as a response to how an individual labels situations as opposed to a situation response per se. The extent to which individuals inappropriately distinguish situational indications as being personally threatening determines their subsequent emotional and behavioral ill-adaptation. Goldfried believed that by attempting to alter the maladaptive cognitive sets that immediately participate when confronted with anxiety-provoking circumstances , people would develop more efficient coping repertoires. Thus, SRR's aim is to train clients in a series of five discrete stages to perceive situational indications more accurately:

(1) Sensitivity to conditions with fear, using fictional scenario or role-playing;

(2) self-assessing of the level of subjective anxiety;

(3) Distress control-causing cognition;

(4) Logical reassessment of these maladjusted cognitions; and

(5) Evaluating one's subjective level of fear after a reasonable reassessment;

Techniques include methods of relaxation, conduct rehearsal, in vivo assignments, modelling, and bibliotherapy. As an approach to coping skills, SRR's ultimate goal is to provide clients with the personal resources to deal with future life stresses independently.

SRR is one of several approaches designed and tested by behavioral researchers for training in coping skills. Some of these treatment packages have received more research attention than others; many are similar in terms of their underlying rationale and therapeutic strategies and while SSR has conceptual integrity, it has not been investigated as extensively as other training programs for coping skills. Nevertheless, it represents one of the first attempts to design an operational self-control treatment model to improve the generalization of treatment through the use of general coping skills training that we believe to be applicable in a variety of stress-provoking situations.

The anxiety management training (AMT) program of Suinn and Richardson (1971) represents another effort at self-control, applied to anxiety problem. AMT, a non-specific anxiety control approach, was designed to provide a short-term coping skills training program for clients that is applicable to a wide range of problem areas. The model 's assumption underlying AMT is that anxiety is an acquired drive which has the properties of generalizing stimulation. Anxiety-related autonomic responses act as signals that facilitate and maintain avoidance behaviour. Clients can be conditioned with responses that eliminate anxiety through the process of reciprocal inhibition to respond to these discriminative signals. AMT 's aim is therefore to teach clients to use relaxation and competency skills to control their anxiety feelings.

AMT stresses the reduction of fear without the actual anxiety-provoking stimulus being given extra consideration. Clients get instruction in intense muscle relaxation at the first level of therapy. Thereafter, customers are instructed to visualize anxiety-inciting scenes, then practice their relaxation skills and/or imagine competently responding to stimuli (Suinn, 1972). The recovery plan includes a number of anxiety-arousing scenarios that may be linked to actual issues encountered by clients.

Empirical evidence surrounding AMT has slowly emerged. In a randomized clinical trial, AMT had been shown to be superior to a defined control group (Suinn, 1995). Yet other data is sparse. AMT remained a less well-developed cognitive-behavioral approach than it would otherwise be, despite the lack of study.

The movement towards therapy approaches advocating a self-control theory inspired the development of a self-control depression paradigm by Rehm (1977). Rehm's work was largely guided by the general model of self-regulation proposed by Kanfer (1970, 1971), which explains the persistence of certain behaviors in the absence of reinforcement in terms of an adaptive self-control system of a closed-loop feedback. Kanfer suggested that the self-regulation involve three interconnected processes: self-monitoring, self-assessment and self-reinforcement. Rehm adapted this model to conceptualize depression symptoms as the result of one or some combination of six self-control behavioral deficits. Potential deficits in the self-monitoring phase include selective monitoring of negative events and immediate, versus delayed, behavioral consequences. Self-assessment deficiencies cover strict self-assessment requirements and unreliable accountability attributions. Deficits involving insufficient self-reward and excessive self-punishment can be observed in depressed individuals during the self-reinforcement phase. According to Rehm (1981), clinical depression 's varied symptom profile is a function of different subsets of those deficits. It is postulated that the occurrence of a depressive episode is a joint function of the degree of stress experienced and the self-control skills available to cope with the stressful situation.

Fuchs and Rehm (1977) created the initial therapy kit based on the Rehm (1977) concept of depression. 'Self-control therapy' means the sequential application of Kanfer's (1970, 1971) three self-regulatory processes as adapted by Rehm: 'The hypothesis is that each can be conceptualized as a therapy module and that self-assessment is based on self-monitoring and self-reinforcement is based on self-assessment.' Each of the six self-control deficits is described over the course of treatment, with a focus on how a particular deficit is causally related to depression and what can be done to remedy the deficit. To teach clients self-control skills, a variety of clinical strategies are used, including group discussion with the therapist, overt and covert reinforcement, behavioral assignments, self-monitoring, and modeling. Rehm's (1977) self-control model 's appeal lies in its integration of a range of cognitive and behavioral variables that are focused exclusively on other depression models. Additionally, Rehm 's theory offers a systematic explanation of how each of the various depressive symptoms is correlated with a particular feature of self-control. From a broader perspective, as a general model of psychopathology, this model of self-control appears to have potential. Unfortunately, no research has been done into the ability of Rehm's theoretical approach to generalize to other clinical disorders. However, it would seem a worthwhile effort to develop comprehensive self-control therapy.

Stress Inoculation Training

As with many of his colleagues in the 1970s, Meichenbaum formed an interest in the transition to multi-component coping strategies as a theoretically useful therapeutic method. Following a review of the stress literature Meichenbaum, Turk, and Burstein (1975) incorporated several guidelines in the development of a treatment program for coping skills. These included the need for flexibility, sensitivity to individual differences, the need to use provocative stimuli to encourage skills utilization, and progressive exposure to threatening situations (Meichenbaum, 1977). Meichenbaum emphasized the regular development of coping skills and emphasized the value of studying how to deal with low, achievable stress levels as a way of promoting the continuation and generalization of therapies. Stress inoculation training, the behavioral analog of Orne's (1965) model of immunization, incorporated the guidelines gleaned by Meichenbaum and his associates from their review of the literature. The rationale behind this approach assumes that clients who learn ways to cope with moderate stress levels are "inoculated" against uncontrollable stress levels.

Meichenbaum and Cameron (1973) did three-stage operationalization of stress inoculation preparation. The first stage is educational, and involves teaching on the nature of stressful reactions. The second stage involves a series of behavioral and cognitive coping skills, including relaxation exercises, coping with self-statements, and self-reinforcement.

The client is exposed to a wide range of stressors during the final stage of application training to rehearse his or her newly acquired coping skills.

Researchers have applied the stress inoculation teaching technique to a number of issues since its implementation in 1973, including fear, frustration and discomfort. These studies resulted in a detailed clinical guidebook (Meichenbaum, 1985) as well as a large body of trials. However, as Jaremko (1979) observed, research into stress inoculation training has introduced a considerable degree of variation in procedures. In this regard, Jaremko suggested an updated methodological model with the goal of bringing greater clarity to the existing work and increasing the "usability" of this technique as a clinical method. As with other multi-component treatment programs, further empirical investigations remain necessary to demonstrate the usefulness of the individual components of treatment employed in stress inoculation training.

Nonetheless, stress inoculation training has been widely used as a therapeutic approach for generalized coping skills development.

Problem-Solving Therapy

In 1971, D'Zurilla and Goldfried published an article proposing the application of problem — solving behavior modification theory and research. With the aim of facilitating "generalized" changes in behaviour, D'Zurilla and Gold-fried conceptualized problem-solving therapy as a form of self-control training, emphasizing the importance of training the client to function as their own therapist. Its authors sum up the rationale behind this approach as follows:

Ineffectiveness in dealing with problematic situations is often a necessary and sufficient condition for an emotional or behavioral disorder requiring psychological treatment, along with its personal and social consequences. General effectiveness may be facilitated most effectively by training individuals in general practices or skills that would allow them to deal independently with the critical problem situations they face in their daily lives.

According to D'Zurilla and Goldfried (1971), "problem solving" refers to an overt or cognitive process that provides a variety of effective alternatives to cope with a problem situation and increases the likelihood of choosing the most effective response available. D'Zurilla and Goldfried identified five overlapping stages as representative of the problem-solving process, drawing on a large body of research on the fundamental operations involved in effective problem-solving:

(1) General or "fixed" orientation;

(2) The definition and formulation of problems,

(3) Alternate Generation,

(4) In making choices, and

(5) Check-in.

Training in problem-solving involves teaching these basic skills to clients and guide their application in real trouble situations.

Spivack and Shure (1974) initiated a systematic investigation into the effectiveness of a problem-solving approach to the treatment. The model proposed by these researchers for interpersonal cognitive problem-solving (ICPS) involves essentially the same skills outlined by D'Zurilla and Goldfried (1971).

According to Spivack, Platt and Shure (1976), the ability to successfully solve interpersonal issues is:

(1) To recognize the range of possible situations of concern in the social environment;

(2) Developing multiple alternatives to interpersonal problems;

(3) Planning a series of steps necessary to attain a given objective;

(4) Predicting the short- and long-term consequences of a given alternative; and

(5) To identify the elements of motivation related to one's actions and those of others.

ICPS training was most commonly used with preschoolers and children with emotional disorders. ICPS training programs generally include discussion and structured activities that involve hypothetical and actual interpersonal problem situations designed to teach problem-solving skills. Despite numerous methodological problems, Spivack 's work and his colleagues have led to a growing interest in the potential of problem-solving therapies.

D'Zurilla and Nezu (1982) conducted an early review of the applications of the original problem-solving model of D'Zurilla and Goldfried (1971) in adult clinical populations and concluded that a relationship exists between problem-solving skills and psychopathology.

The clinical intervention goals D'Zurilla and Goldfried (1971) recommended stimulated the development of a number of problem-solving therapies. Problem-solving therapies have now been developed in several fields including stress management and prevention (D'Zurilla, 1990), depression (Nezu, 1986), anger management (Crick & Dodge, 1994), and cancer coping (Nezu, Nezu, Friedman, Faddis, & Houts, 1998). A general problem-solving approach was an outstanding addition to the catalog of available surgical techniques (D'Zurilla&Nezu, 1999). The flexibility and pragmatism of these approaches is likely to continue to attract clinicians' attention in search of comprehensive treatment programmes.

Structural and Constructivist Psychotherapy

Guidano and Liotti (1983) introduced psychotherapy with a structural approach. Following a comprehensive study of numerous literatures, including behavioral therapy, social learning theory, evolutionary epistemology, cognitive psychology, psycho-dynamic theory and cognitive therapy, Guidano and Liotti concluded that to understand the complete complexity of emotional disorder and subsequently develop an adequate model of psychotherapy, development appreciation and activity

The structural model of cognitive dysfunction used by Guidano and Liotti (1983) borrowed heavily from Bowlby's (1977) attachment theory. They suggested that relationships with significant others (i.e., parents) determine a child's self-image development and provide continuous confirmation and strengthening of that self-image. It is assumed that the definition of the "self" coordinates and integrates cognitive growth and emotional differentiation. If the self-concept is distorted or rigid, the individual is unable to effectively assimilate life experiences, which leads to maladjustment and emotional distress, cognitive dysfunction being the end product. It is assumed that different anomalous attachment patterns match different clinical syndromes.

In subsequent writings, Guidano expanded the original formulation of Guidano and Liotti (1987, 1991). These writings expanded the idea that problem behaviors are thought to be the consequence of the cognitive organization of an individual (i.e., the causal theories, basic assumptions, and tacit inference rules that determine the content of the thought). In the face of a constantly demanding climate, the individual is viewed as trying to sustain a single dysfunctional cognitive structure. Thus, psychotherapy's ultimate goal is to modify those cognitive structures. To make therapy successful, the therapist starts by identifying and modifying superficial cognitive structures which in turn lead to the identification and modification of deeper cognitive structures (i.e., the patient's implicit causal theories). This therapeutic strategy bears a close resemblance to Beck's cognitive therapy, which begins with the evaluation of the automatic thoughts of the patient and then leads to the specification of the basic assumptions underlying these ideas. However, a significant contrast between the founders of relational psychotherapy and Beck is the emphasis on a postrationalist ideology placed by the former writers. Whereas Beck and related authors make a philosophical assumption that there is an outside world that can be perceived accurately or distorted, Guidano 's later writings in particular make it clear that he is increasingly less concerned with the "truth value" of cognitive structures than with the "validity value" or coherence of these structures:

Therefore, adaptation is the ability to transform perturbation resulting from interaction with the world into information relevant to one's experiential order. Maintaining adaptive adequacy essentially means reserving one's sense of self by continuously transforming rather than merely corresponding to the perceived world. This explains why in modern evolutionary epistemology the notion of the efficacy of information systems has become far more significant than that of their validity.

When addressing psychotherapy as a pragmatic method, relational therapists respond to the contrast between the scientist's scientific problem-solving approach and the patient's approach: "Therapists will encourage patients to disengage from those ingrained assumptions and perceptions and accept them as hypotheses and ideas, subject to disproof, validation, and logical challenge." This comparison is similar to the one Mahoney (1977) has drawn in his approach to personal research. The psychological armory is composed of a number of clinical tests and cognitive strategies from which the psychiatrist chooses a selection of effective methods for an individual case. They include techniques such as imaginary flooding, systematic desensitization, training in assertiveness, training in coping skills, problem-solving and rational restructuring. The final stage of the therapeutic process is conceptualized as a "personal revolution" in which the patient, having rejected his or her old view of himself and the world, is in a state of transformation and is setting up a new, more adaptive system of beliefs.

Those familiar with Beck et al. (1979), Ellis (1962), Mahoney (1977), and other cognitive-behavioral advocates will recognize the many parallels between their writings and the structural approach to therapy. Nevertheless, the distinction between rational and postrational approaches is important and has been further amplified in the work of people who refer to their work as constructivist psychotherapy (Mahoney, 1991; 1995; Neimeyer, 1993, 1995; Neimeyer & Mahoney, 1995). Constructivist therapy takes the individual's view as an imperfect personal scientist, who uses cognitive constructs to make sense out of the world's experiences and choices. From this view, a primary therapeutic function includes recognizing personal patterns and understanding how significance is linked to experience. There is less focus on the content of what is being thought of (e.g., as opposed to Beck's [1976] work, in which a cognition typology is associated with different emotional states), and more focus on the process of making meaning and connections between experiments. Therapy is, therefore, less involved in corrective exercises about what is being thought, and more in facilitative exercises that emphasize the thinking process and meaning-generation.

Constructivist therapy has a close affinity with hermeneutical philosophical schools, and psychological approaches to narrative and discourse. Nonetheless, within constructivism there are more or less "radical" approaches. In the extreme viewpoint of constructivist therapy, referred to as discursive critique or "true constructivism," the epistemological stance that truth actually resides in the individual's mind and that the only criteria for mental wellbeing is the coherence of that mind set. Individuals are regarded as contextual, temporary, cultural, sexual, and otherwise positioned in relation to other persons. As such, predetermined concepts of health and disease, such as the diagnostic nomenclature traditionally associated with mental disorders, lose their significance, and treatment is no longer a process to help people recover from their diagnosed disorders. The relation between constructivist therapies and other CBTs begins to break down at this extreme. Others have also asked how conceptually consistent constructivist approaches are with CBTs: "We believe that some scholars proposed complete convergence of cognitive and constructivist models. The intellectual challenges must be faced. Other authors (e.g., Held, 1995) who criticized the movement in psychotherapy towards constructivist schools of thought suggested that therapies should turn "back to reality."

The final chapter of the constructivist approaches to psychotherapy clearly still has to be written. However, it is not lost to us that many former advocates of traditional cognitive and CBTs later advocated the use of treatments based on constructivist principles in whole or in part (Mahoney, 1991; Meichenbaum, 1994; Young, 1994). It remains to be seen to what extent these therapies are considered part of the cognitive-behavioral movement, or move away into antithetical and alternative therapy approaches.

"Third-Wave" Cognitive-Behavioral Therapy

The "third wave" has been a recent trend in the field of CBT. This group of therapies is most often associated with acceptance and commitment therapy. ACT and related models focus not so much on the accuracy of perception but on the functional utility of various ways of thinking and acting. As with the structural psychotherapies, the emphasis is placed on the process of interacting with the world rather than on the content of what is being thought or done. That said, Steven Hayes, the originator of ACT, would argue that this approach is radically behavioral in that it emphasizes action to maximize mental health and worldwide adaptation. Therefore, as is true with the other CBTs, there is an emphasis on both thinking and action.

One way that ACT differs from many of the other CBTs is that the cognitive focus is not only on specific situations, or the assessment and meaning attached to different experiences, but also on the evaluation process itself. Thus, there is a focus on the "metacognitive" processes, such as worrying about worry or depression distress. Associated with this focus on meta-cognition is a concomitant focus on "consciousness," being aware of the appraisal process for events, emotions, and other ideas.

Another dimension of the paradigm that underlies some of the third-wave models is that the transition cycle can take place in different ways. While problem-solving, self-control and cognitive restructuring approaches to CBT emphasize the need to evaluate cognition and behavior and correct these phenomena when associated with emotional distress or problems, the third-wave approach suggests that sometimes the "change" needed is to recognize that meta-cognitive processes are at fault; The ACT therapist explicitly reinforces processes for accepting difficult situations, even while committing to doing what the patient wants to fulfill his or her life. A common question is: "What should you do when you were? "With the assistance of the therapist to help the patient do just that. It is further argued that the promoted constructive and beneficial behaviour can be compounded favorably by the patient's experience, and in this mechanism the desire to alter "the issue" is removed.

The third-wave therapies, as described by Hayes and others, are part of the cognitive-behavioral tradition because of their emphasis on cognitive assessment and behavioral change. However, it is clear that the approach of these therapies to pain, anxiety, and issues is fundamentally different from that of other CBTs, and that their connection to CBT "mainstream" needs to be discerned. Additionally, while encouraging, the evidence base relating to the outcome for these treatments is relatively sparse.

Diversity and Similarities among the Cognitive-Behavioral Therapies

There are a wide range of cognitive-behavioral approaches, as the previous chronology of cognitive-behavioral models of psychopathology and rehabilitation indicates. The bases of all these approaches share the three basic assumptions we discussed earlier in this chapter regarding the position of mediation. Briefly stated, the "mediative position" is that cognitive activity mediates the individual's responses to his or her environment, and to some extent, dictates the individual's degree of adjustment or maladjustment. The CBTs hold a view that psychological improvement can be achieved by modifying idiosyncratic, unhealthy way of thought as a direct result of the mediational presumption. In addition, many of the cognitive-behavioral methods are based on behavioral principles and techniques in the conduct of therapy due to the behavioral heritage, and many of the cognitive-behavioral models rely to some extent on behavioral change assessment to document therapeutic progress.

Beyond these central assumptions concerning the mediated nature of therapeutic change, there are a number of commonalities among limited sets of CBTs. For example, Kendall and Kriss (1983) suggested that five dimensions could be used to characterize CBTs: the theoretical orientation of the therapeutic approach and the theoretical goal of change, various aspects of the client-therapist relationship, the cognitive goal of change, the type of evidence used for cognitive evaluation, and the degree of self-control emphasis on pa. The scheme they've developed is helpful in defining the parallels and disparities between the various CBTs. Despite Kendall and Kriss covering the topic, it also appears that other commonalities can be identified between approaches which are not theoretically central. One commonality among the different CBTs, for example, is their time-limited nature. In direct difference from long-term psychoanalytic treatment, CBTs seek to affect immediate improvement, most sometimes with limited, predetermined clinical touch times. Many of the counseling guides published for CBTs prescribe medication in the 12–16 session scale.

The time-limited essence of CBT is due to the fact that almost all implementations of this general therapy approach include particular issues. While this commonality is by no means a criticism of the different CBTs, and although there has also been some recent interest in trans-diagnostic approaches to psycho-pathology and treatment, the problem-focused nature of cognitive-behavioral interventions explains in part the time constraints commonly set in these therapy approaches. Nevertheless, the use of such treatments for particular conditions and issues is a legacy of the reliance on the gathering of result results through behaviour counseling and the insistence on remedying real, predefined issues. Therefore, rather than being a disadvantage of CBTs, adapting such treatments to particular conditions acts as evidence of the growing need for treatment outcomes to be reported in full. Focusing on specific issues also allows the measurement of the therapeutic limits of these different approaches and the potential for selecting the most effective therapy for the problem of a given patient.

The third commonality among cognitive — behavioral approaches is the belief that customers are, in a sense, the architects of their own misfortune and thus have control over their thoughts and actions. The type of patient problems identified for cognitive-behavioral interventions clearly reflects this assumption. The most frequently cited appropriate issues include "neurotic" conditions (e.g. problems with anxiety, depression, and anger), self-control issues (e.g., overeating, behavioral management problems, child dysfunction), and general problem-solving abilities. Both kinds of complications make it tenable to presume care of the patient. The emphasis on the patient as the active participant of his or her own life is a prevalent theme, particularly of broad approaches to therapy, such as the constructivist models.

Another factor which a number of CBTs share is linked to the presumption of patient control. This commonality relates to the fact that many CBTs are either explicitly or implicitly educational by nature. Many of the therapeutic approaches include the therapist who teaches the therapeutic model to the patient, and many also include an explanation of the rationale for any interventions that are being carried out. This type of educational interaction between the therapist and the patient is one facet that is shared by the different CBTs, and that again distinguishes them from other therapy schools. Contrast conventional psychoanalytic treatment, in which the therapist gives explanations to the client, or proactive family therapy, in which the therapist can also suggest that the client does the reverse of what the clinical purpose is in a "paradoxical" technique.

The underlying target set by many cognitive-behavioral therapists is closely linked to the developmental cycle frequently found in CBTs: that the patient not only overcomes the treatment problem through counseling but also understands more about the counseling itself. Therefore, in case the patient has a recurrence of the condition, he or she may have other coping abilities to cope with the condition itself. In some of the CBTs, the desire for patients to learn about the therapy process is brought to its logical conclusion, and time in therapy is spent reviewing the therapeutic concepts and skills that patients have learned throughout the course of therapy, so that they can later use them in maintenance or preventive way.

CBTs may seem to have so many commonalities that differentiations between them are more illusory than real. However, in addition, Kendall and Kriss (1983) presented an excellent structure for the recognition of discrepancies between the different approaches. Moreover, only the short summary of the different CBTs given in this chapter reveals a very significant variety in cognitive-behavioral therapists' styles and strategies. Therefore, it is no more acceptable to say that a single cognitive-behavioral approach exists than to say that there is one monolithic psychoanalytic treatment. As the chapters in this volume show, within the overarching definition of the cognitive-behavioral approach, many different facets of cognition-behavioral processes can be addressed, identified, and altered. The variety of the CBTs, though undeniably current, appeals between the advocates of the different methods for more definitional and theoretical debate. There are at least two fields where more analysis and study are needed to better distinguish the various interventions classified as "cognitive — behavioral" the aims of psychological improvement, and the complexity of the modalities of the therapy strategies.

Although CBTs share the mediation approach and thus all target "cognitions" to change the variety of specific labels and cognition descriptions seen in cognitive-behavioral literature is truly overwhelming. A partial list of the various concepts applicable to cognitive structures and mechanisms includes "cognitions," "thinks," "beliefs," "attitudes," "ideas," "assumptions," "attributions," "rules for living," "self-statements," "cognitive hallucinations," "expectancies," "notions," "stream of consciousness," "plot," "narratives," "ideas," "internal interpretations," "illusions," "self-efficacy predivisions" Where words are used across psychology fields the interpretation may not be the same, so the end effect may be semant uncertainty. For example, the use of the notion of "schema" is fraught with potential difficulty, as the concept was first developed within cognitive psychology (Neisser, 1967) and later applied to social cognition (Markus, 1977), then applied to clinical problems as well. Only a fast analysis of the term's various implementations shows that while the meaning of the "schema" definition is preserved in all its different uses, there are many idiosyncratic implementations. Thus, while the elaboration of different specific cognitive processes and constructs is useful, it is important for theorists to precisely define constructs, and for others in the field to subscribe to those definitions. An improvement in consistency would serve to illuminate the landscape of cognitive-behavioral science and may also support researchers whose focus is in cognitive performance. In this regard, it is clear that cognitive evaluation is seriously hindered by a lack of consistent descriptions of cognitive anomalies, and it is equally clear that more cognitive evaluation efforts are required to better capture the existence and mechanism of improvement during CBT.

In terms of modality-specific techniques, a second area where further delineation of different approaches to CBT may be possible. Cognitive — behavioral practitioners have been highly creative in approach development, introducing several forms to the therapeutic armamentarium. However, in doing so, it is not always clear what form of technique is being introduced (i.e., whether it is a common and non-specific technique or a process unique to the modality). While it may reasonably be argued that such distinctions are not important in practice , it is important from a theoretical perspective to know what limitations different theorists place on their therapy models. Process research that actually records and analyzes therapeutic interventions underpinned by different therapeutic models, while often suggested, has not yet developed well. This type of research has the potential to greatly add to our knowledge of the extent to which different therapy descriptions translate into different clinical practices.

Lastly, another field of study that can be extended profitably is that which explores implementations of various CBT modes to various presenting problems. It may become possible to suggest preferred methods of treatment for specific patient problems by contrasting different approaches in the context of different problems. This matching of problems with therapies would not only represent a practical advantage over current clinical practice, but would also allow a better understanding of the mechanisms of change within each type of intervention, and within different types of patient problems.

Clearly, the CBT sector has grown significantly since its emergence in the sixties and seventies. There are now a number of identifiable cognitive-behavioral models, and generally strong is the demonstrated effectiveness of these methods. The continued focus on outcome research has enabled cognitive-behavioral theorists and therapists to make steady progress in research and practice, and will certainly lead to continuous improvements in the future. Some of the most pressing areas requiring further conceptualization and research include the definition of cognitive phenomena (both at the level of construction and process) and the procedural overlap between the currently existing variety of CBTs. Another area emerging for the field is dissemination. Considerable progress in the field is likely to be seen over the next decade.

CHAPTER FIVE

The Effectiveness of Cognitive Behavioral Therapy

Mood Disorders

Unipolar Depression

In the CBT treatment outcome literature, unipolar depression has received considerable attention and several meta-analyzes have been published on the subject. Gloaguen et al. included studies that contained at least one CT group and one comparison group in their analyses; the CT treatments had to either follow Beck's CT manual or refer to Beck 's model explicitly. They also allowed participants to be selected at random. Comparison groups included untreated controls; waiting lists, pharmacotherapy, and conditions of behavioral therapy; and a heterogeneous set of "other therapies" in the 48 studies they considered. Gloaguen et al . found clear evidence of the total effectiveness of CT, and the supremacy of CT over other therapies, but they cautioned that these latter results would be viewed with caution as they did not reach the homogeneity between trials. Their results also demonstrated the superiority of CT over antidepressants, and the equivalence of behavior therapy (BT) and CT, this time with high homogeneity between trials. We also observed that antidepressant relapse levels surpassed CT at 1- to 2-year follow-up, though this finding was reached purely by measuring the number of relapses. Gloaguen et al . (1998) did not find any of their postulated moderators (initial Beck Depression Inventory [BDI] score, sex, age) meaningful. They concluded that in individuals with mild or moderate depression, equivalence to BT and superiority to antidepressants, CT shows absolute effectiveness.

Wampold, Minami, Baskin, and Tierney were unhappy about the Gloaguen et al. (1998) classification of "other therapies." They claimed that the merger of bona fide and non-bona fide psychotherapies into the category of "other therapies" could explain their results in relation to CT. They explored this hypothesis by re-analyzing data from the Gloaguen et al . (1998). They found CT to be roughly as effective as other bona fide treatments, but superior to non-bona fide treatments. We concluded that all bona fide psychiatric therapies are similarly successful for depression.

In patients with moderate to severe depression, DeRubeis et al . (2005) conducted an RCT comparing CT and pharmacotherapy and found that 24 CT sessions delivered by experienced therapists were as effective as pharmacotherapy. Long-term findings showed that patients who had received CT were slightly less likely than those who stopped treatment to relapse over a 12-month cycle, and had relapse levels similar to those who resumed treatment.

Segal, Vincent, and Levitt (2002) concluded that combining anti-depressant drugs with CT could be more effective than either of the treatment modalities alone, especially for people with more severe depression. However, this question may become moot, as a recent meta-analysis found virtually no difference in the outcome of treatment between patients with moderate levels of initial depression receiving a pill — placebo and those receiving antidepressants, and relatively small effects for patients initially severely deprimed.

Bipolar Disorder

Several research papers explored the effectiveness of therapy for bipolar disorder, but no meta-analyzes have been done yet. Medicines remain the first line of treatment for bipolar disorder, but psychotherapy can be an effective adjunctive medication of bipolar disorder due to the shortcomings inherent of pharmacotherapy, such as inadequate adherence, regular recurrences of symptoms, sub-syndromic exacerbations and the persistence of severe functional impairments. Psychotherapy can improve early response approaches, tolerance, quality of life, and the preventive impact of family and social support systems; increase patient awareness and ability to regulate episodes; promote everyday schedule maintenance and sleep-wake cycles; and increase adherence to medication.

Zaretsky, Rizvi, and Parikh (2007) reviewed RCTs for psycho-education, family-focused therapy, brief CBT interventions (e.g., psycho-education, homework, and self-monitoring), CBT for bipolar disorder, CBT for prevention of relapse (e.g., psycho-education, CT for depression, identification of relapse and prevention prodromes, and routine stabilisation), interpersonal therapy, and social rhythm th. They concluded that manualised, short-term, specifically targeted psychotherapies as adjuncts to medication offer consistent benefits. CBT, family-focused treatment, and psycho-education have shown the most comprehensive outcomes of relapse reduction, whereas behavioral counseling and CBT have treated persistent depression symptoms more successfully.

Miklowitz and Otto (2006), Gonzalez-Pinto et al . (2004), and Colom and Vieta (2004) generally agree that in treating bipolar disorder, psychotherapy is an effective adjunct to the medication. Jones (2004) indicated that the success of psychosocial treatments can be overestimated due to the unregulated complexity and low consistency of most of the treatment efficacy study, while he acknowledged that progress has been made in improving therapeutic adjunctive strategies. He also commented that different interventions affect depression and mania differently and that some approaches may be more effective for one phase of the disorder or another. Gonzalez-Pinto et al . (2004) have cautioned that potentially helpful treatments for latent depressive symptoms and bipolar disorder in the early stages of manic symptoms could be harmful. Colom and Vieta (2004) noted that most psycho-social interventions are similar in that they include a psycho-educational component, and that most have shown similarly positive outcomes. CBT has shown efficacy on some measures up to 9 years post-treatment, but heterogeneity across studies does not allow long-term statements to be conclusive.

Anxiety Disorders
Specific Phobia

Although the anxiety conditions are typically well described in the literature on the treatment effect, the literature is fairly scarce on particular phobias. Outside of trials carried out in non-clinical environments and due to experimental shortcomings such as insufficient sampling sizes, unpredictable architectures, and inconsistency between solely therapeutic and CBT therapies, results that remain are mostly of low quality. There was no meta-analysis on the subject, while Choy et al. wrote a detailed systematic overview of clinical findings. They used a "best proof" approach and found that therapies are not equally successful, and have differential effectiveness across subtypes of phobia. The BTs were most commonly accepted, with good acute results for in vivo treatment in most subtypes of phobia. However, in vivo use was associated with comparatively high dropout levels and poor acceptance of therapy. Systematic desensitization demonstrated more modest effectiveness, and, despite similar outcomes for height phobia and flight phobia, virtual reality treatment was found to be a theoretically appropriate alternative to in vivo exposure.

Choy et al . (2006) showed that in treating claustrophobia, the use of cognitive reinforcement, either alone or in conjunction with in vivo treatment, was successful. In addition, CT could be a strong alterative to in vivo treatment for claustrophobia, they proposed. While CT has not been found to improve the outcomes of animal or flying phobias in vivo exposure, the authors speculated that this may have been due to ceiling effects given the high level of in vivo exposure efficacy. CT has also shown beneficial effects as a solo treatment for dental and flying phobias, and gains for CT combined with in vivo exposure for the one animal study (spiders) have been maintained at 12 months. The results of CT alone for claustrophobia were also shown to be long-lasting, but less so for flight or dental phobias. Two other research showed that participants viewed therapies that combined cognitive constructs and features of the behaviour as less aversive and/or less invasive than exposure-only interventions.

Social Anxiety Disorder

"Social Anxiety Disorder" (SAD), otherwise known as social phobia, has received considerable attention in the literature on treatment for CBT. Six meta-analyzes and several review articles have been published on the subject, to our knowledge (e.g., Fresco & Heimberg, 2001; Heimberg, 2002; Rodebaugh et al . , 2004; Rowa & Antony, 2005). The new meta-analysis specifically contrasts pharmacotherapy, CBT, or a mixture of the two in 16 stress disorder trials, six SAD tests, and two general anxiety disorder trials (Bandelow, Seidler — Brandler, Becker, Wedekind, & Rüther, 2007). CBT included cognitive strategies, fear reduction and perception interventions implemented in a group or adult style. Both therapies for SAD resulted in significant amounts of pre- and post-treatment effects; clinicians ranked the largest improvements in pharmacotherapy from pre- to post-treatment, while patients viewed the combination intervention as the most successful. In post-treatment pharmacotherapy alone had a minimal advantage over CBT alone. Preliminary evidence for CBT was also given in conjunction with pharmacotherapy, based on two trials. Bandelow et al . found conflicting outcomes with follow-up evidence that analyzed CBT and pharmacotherapy effectiveness.

Rodebaugh et al . (2004) summarized the results of five meta-analyzes (Chambless & Hope, 1996; Fedoroff & Taylor , 2001; Feske&Chambless, 1995; Gould, Buckmeister, Pollack, Otto, & Yap, 1997; Taylor, 1996) and reported, in all meta-analyzes, moderate to large controlled effect sizes for CBT. They also found that for CBT, moderate to large uncontrolled effect sizes within a group were reported, similar to findings from Bandelow et al . (2007). In fact, they noted that both trials demonstrated CBT results sustained at follow-up, if not slight additional progress. While most meta-analyzes included studies with 2–6 month follow-up assessments, Feske and Chambless (1995) and Chambless and Hope (1996) included studies with follow-up assessments of up to 12 months. CBT 's total usefulness with respect to social phobia has been well-founded.

The overall usefulness of CBT for social phobia is a little hard to determine. Federoff and Taylor (2001) examined medicines, exposure, cognitive restructuring, exposure plus cognitive restructuring, social skills training, and relaxation applied, and found medicines were the most consistently effective treatments. At the other hand, Gould et al . (1997) indicated that CBT, pharmacotherapy, and their mixture both varied greatly from one another. Exposure, cognitive restructuring, cognitive restructuring plus exposure, and training in social skills also seem to be noticeably different in efficacy.

On the basis of these meta-analyses, variations between types of cognitive — behavioral therapies are difficult to establish. The only substantial variation between therapies, as examined in Rodebaugh et al . (2004), preferred exposure plus cognitive adjustment over placebo (Taylor, 1996), but only by clinician ranking, not by client self-report. Gould et al . (1997) found that treatment, whether alone or combined with cognitive enhancement, resulted in the highest impact sizes among its treatments. Feske and Chambless (1995), unlike the previous researchers, differentiated between CBT and exposure, defining CBT as cognitive restructuring plus exposure. They concluded that both exposure and CBT were equally effective. Rodebaugh et al . (2004) noted that CBT, which incorpo-rates cognitive adjustment and treatment, can be best supported if one recognizes nonsignificant differences between effect sizes.

Most meta — analyzes looked at dropout rates. Although Gould et al . (1997) found no statistically significant difference in dropout rates between pharmacotherapy, the combined condition, and CBT, the respective attrition rates of 13.7, 6.7, and 10.7 per cent suggested that the presence of CBT moderates drug attrition alone. In comparison, Fedoroff and Taylor (2001) found negligible variations in their 11 conditions. However, attrition rates varied considerably, from about 6% for waiting-list control to about 23% for benzodiazepines and monoamine oxidase inhibitors, with cognitive restructuring plus exposure falling to nearly 19%. Taylor (1996) found equally non-significant dropout risk variations, ranging from 5.7% for waiting list management to 18% for cognitive rehabilitation plus access.

Finally, Rodebaugh et al . (2004) found no differences between CBT formats individually and grouply. Gould et al. calculated cost projections, and determined that group CBT was the most cost-effective treatment option choice. Feske and Chamb-less (1995) also examined the issue of "dose-response" for CBT and investigated whether treatment gains increased compared to exposure with an increasing number of CBT sessions. They found that treatment length only affected treatment outcomes for exposure, resulting in improved outcomes due to a greater number of sessions.

Obsessive–Compulsive Disorder

CBT and pharmacotherapy were established as the two treatments of choice for obsessive – compulsive disorder (OCD), with exposure and ritual, or response, prevention (ERP) being the most effective form of CBT, according to a review article (Allen, 2006). While exposure-based therapies are called therapeutic, they are almost always paired with cognitive strategies, because cognitive interventions are used to empower clients and help them handle the exposure. Therefore Allen refers interchangeably to ERP and CBT. Abramowitz et al . examined dropout rates and found that the inclusion of cognitive techniques with behavioral experiments reduces discontinuation of treatment , suggesting that CBT is more acceptable to OCD patients than ERP.

Allen (2006) contended among the psychotherapies that CBT (with ERP) is the only treatment that has proved effective. He further came to the conclusion that the combination of pharmacotherapy and CBT in individuals with comorbid depression and OCD is more effective than CBT alone. However, he also maintained that preliminary research indicates that CBT in relapse prevention is superior to pharmacotherapy, particularly after discontinuation of medication. Lastly, Allen warned that many people with OCD remain symptomatic after treatment, and that as a result of treatment, many individuals do not even experience improvements, often because they are unable to meet the treatment terms.

At least three meta-analyzes on the use of CBT in the treatment of OCD were conducted. These meta-analysis' overall pattern is consistent with the previous synopsis. Eddy, Dutra, Bradley, and Westen (2004) recently examined ERP, CBT, and CT separately, together with a range of pharmacological interventions. They determined that both psychotherapy and pharmacotherapy result in significant declines in OCD symptoms as reflected by unstandardized effect sizes, significant percentages of patients improving with treatment, and significant declines in symptoms from pre- to post-treatment treatment. They specified that the treatments based on behavior were more effective than the interventions based on cognition. They analyzed a small number of studies that included psychotherapy plus pharmacotherapy, and found a more robust effect than for either treatment alone. Given the lack of these trials, they tentatively suggested that combination psychotherapy and pharmacotherapy may be the best treatment for OCD. They noted that insufficient data were available to make any conclusive statements about the sustained effectiveness of psychotherapy, and that their findings suggested that continued pharmacotherapy is needed to maintain long-term gains in treatment. Last, and somewhat disappointingly, they reported that one-third of those who complete a therapy course, and nearly half of those who begin but do not complete the therapy, will not yield expected benefits.

Abramowitz (1997) concluded that cognitive and exposure-based approaches to OCD therapy are similarly successful, which he related to the methodological similarity between the two methods and the theory that they bring about identical processes of improvement. Abramowitz measured the impact size as the uniform disparity between posttest therapies (as compared to Eddy et al . , 2004), while providing more concrete evidence for CBT 's total effectiveness. There was no direct comparison between pharmacotherapy and psychotherapy but several pharmacotherapy types were compared. Most support was found for serotonergic medicines (compared to other classes of antidepressants), which reduced the symptoms of OCD at posttest significantly. Because of insufficient data Abramowitz (1997) did not report follow-up results. Although van Balkom et al . (1994) in their meta-analysis did not directly compare CT with BT, their results did not support equal effectiveness between CT and BT. They found that the only active treatments that were significantly superior to placebo treatment were serotonergic antidepressants, BT and their combination. They also reported that it appeared after visual inspection that the effect sizes remained stable for up to 6 years posttest.

Panic Disorder with or without Agoraphobia

Bandelow et al . (2007) published the most recent meta-analysis to specifically compare pharmacological, psychological, and mixed fear disorder recovery approaches with (PDA) or without (PD) agoraphobia. Researchers observed that on both clinician and self-report scores, pharmacological therapy or CBT alone, and their mixture, yielded broad impact sizes from non- to post-care. Interestingly, for CBT alone, patients reported higher pre – post differences than for drug treatment alone, while clinicians reported the opposite pattern. However, the only statistically significant difference between CBT and pharmacotherapy combined, and pharmacotherapy alone, was between pre- and post-treatment effect sizes. Bandelow et al . reported only a few follow-up studies, producing inconsistent results.

A large meta-analysis of 124 studies also investigated the relative and absolute efficacy of CBT (exposure and cognitive restructuring), pharmacotherapy, and its combination in PD treatment (Mitte, 2005a). For both treatments absolute controlled efficacy has been found. There was little significant benefit from incorporating cognitive elements to BT when evaluating result outcomes for anxiety, but the addition of cognitive elements contributed to an improved reduction in depressive symptoms. CBT has also been related to lower turnover levels relative to BT. This meta-analysis also implied that CBT is at least as effective as pharmacotherapy. In fact,

Mitte reported that while there are some situations where CBT is more suitable, and others where pharmacotherapy is more suitable, there were no significant differences in treatment outcome between CBT, BT, and pharmacotherapy. This study found that, contrary to the results of Bandelow et al . (2007), a combination of CBT and pharmacotherapy was not significantly more effective than CBT alone, either in the short or long term (average 16.8 months). A related meta — analysis found somewhat divergent findings in an earlier study by Gould, Otto and Pollack (1995). Instead of waiting-list controls, they used pill — placebo controls which possibly influenced their outcomes.

Siev and Chambless (2007) conducted a focused meta-analysis of the relative effectiveness of CT (incorporating interceptive exposure) and relaxation therapy (RT) in PD treatment to examine the differential effectiveness of different forms of CBT. They found CT to be superior to RT on all measures related to panic and clinically significant change indices. Oei, Llamas, and Devilly (1999) also conducted a more detailed review of the PDA data available. Through a particular meta-analytic approach, they contrasted the pretreatment, post-treatment and follow-up ratings of a CBT for PDA therapy population on the Fear Questionnaire (FQ), with standard results derived from a neighborhood sample and a college study. They concluded that CBT is effective, as demonstrated by the fact that at post-treatment and follow-up (1 to 16 months post-treatment) the scores of the treatment group on the FQ fell within 2 standard deviations of the mean of a normal population. Researchers concluded that PDA therapy would include presentation in vivo, as avoidance is a distinctive characteristic of the condition. In comparison, they argued that PD is vulnerable to CT or RT because it is synonymous with calamitous benign stimulus misinterpretations.

Landon and Barlow (2004) examined the literature and addressed the therapeutic efficiency of patients with numerous conditions, feasibility, cost effectiveness, obstacles to medication delivery, new advances in CBT, and predictors of success for CBT, in addition to evaluating the actual and relative efficiency of CBT in treating PD/PDA. They find that brief forms of CBT are preferable to other types of psychotherapy, and that for effective recovery, extensive CBT is not required. They determined that CBT individual or group therapy can be applied effectively in a variety of settings by trained clinicians. They also noted that by taking into account the cost of treatment sessions and medications, pharmacotherapy is the most costly of treatment modalities, and CBT has the most desirable cost profile.

Post-traumatic Stress Disorder

Because recommendations have been issued by the National Institute for Clinical Excellence (NICE; National Collaborating Center on Mental Health, 2005), at least two meta-analyzes have been conducted to synthesize the posttraumatic stress disorder (PTSD) recovery outcome study. The most recent study (Bisson et al . , 2007) analyzed the actual and quantitative effectiveness of trauma-focused CBT (TFCBT), stress reduction (SM), other interventions (supportive treatment, nondirective counselling, psychodynamic intervention, and hypnotherapy), CBT community, and desensitization and reprocessing of eye movement (EMDR). The National Behavioral Health Collaboration Center provided training to multiple therapeutic strategies under the TFCBT rubric (e.g. cognitive reprocessing therapy, cognitive restructuring). Thirty-eight experiments were included in the reviews, and findings from both statistical and clinical significance were published. Bisson et al . found that TFCBT demonstrated clinically significant gains in all measures of PTSD symptoms over the waiting list and normal treatment, and insufficient evidence of effectiveness for comorbid depression and anxiety. EMDR has also shown efficacy over the waiting-list and usual care. Although TFCBT and EMDR were not significantly different, the evidence that both TFCBT and EMDR were superior to other therapies was limited. Bisson et al. found no evidence to support the use of "other therapies" for PTSD but found limited evidence for SM and group CBT use. Seidler and Wagner (2006) conducted a meta-analysis of seven trials to explain the relative effectiveness of TFCBT and EMDR. They found no clear evidence of one's superiority over the other, and concluded that the differences observed are probably not clinically significant. Long term outcomes have not been reported.

A meta-analysis of pharmacological and physical interventions for adult PTSD was also conducted by the National Collaborating Center for Mental Health (2005) as part of the review for the NICE guidelines. While some drug therapies demonstrated statistical effectiveness over placebo, when considered an a priori test for a clinically significant effect they worked disappointingly. In one small sample, TFCBT was superior to paroxetine for lowering PTSD frequency on a self-rated scale, for decreasing symptoms of depression on a self-rated scale, and for patient turnover. The evidence was inconsistent as to which method of treatment was more effective in terms of symptoms of depression as assessed by a clinician, and severity of PTSD as assessed by self-report. Long term outcomes have not been reported.

These findings are also in the chronic PTSD sense, not as early approaches implemented immediately after the trauma, or with acute stress disorder. The National Collaborating Center for Mental Health (2005) systematically reviewed early intervention literature which focused on:

(1) Treatments provided to all survivors of trauma within the first month following the incident;

(2) Treatment of people at high risk for persistent PTSD, started within three months of the incident; and

(3) Drug treatment for persons at an acute disorder stage. These results indicate that one-session debriefing (sometimes referred to as "critical incident debriefing") may at best be ineffective immediately after the traumatic incident, and may actually increase the risk of subsequent traumatic symptoms. When delivered 1 to 6 months after the incident, TFCBT decreased post-treatment diagnostic rates as well as self-reported severity of PTSD, anxiety, quality of life, and clinician-rated severity of PTSD. While TFCBT was also more effective in terms of PTSD diagnosis at 9- to 13-month follow-up than waiting-list control, further evidence was inconclusive as there was no clinically significant difference in the severity of PTSD assessed by clinicians. Also, TFCBT was more successful than self-help booklets, calming, or helpful guidance. Lastly, data on early intervention drug treatments were insufficient to provide any conclusive statements about their effectiveness.

Generalized Anxiety Disorder

In 2007 three meta-analyzes on generalized anxiety disorder (GAD) treatments were published. In their study, Bandelow et al . (2007) published only two experiments, and the experiments had limited sample sizes; thus, their findings are not discussed here. Siev and Chambless (2007) used five trials in their study and observed low and non-significant post-treatment unregulated impact sizes between CT and RT on anxiety, anxiety-related cognitions, and depression. Additionally, for all patient classes, the relative chances of experiencing clinically meaningful improvement following diagnosis were small and did not vary. First, the dropout figures were approximately equal.

Hunot et al. (2007) found that patients assigned to CBT were more likely to receive post-treatment behavioral outcomes than people subjected to therapy as normal or waiting list monitors. CBT has showed greater total effectiveness in post-treatment effects of fear, stress , and depression than the normal or waiting-list management therapy. Data were insufficient to determine the absolute efficacy of CBT over the long term. The comparative efficacy of CBT and psychodynamic therapy was limited to one study, though fairly broad, which showed that patients undergoing CBT were more likely to display a therapeutic response and a decrease in symptoms of anxiety and depression than those seeking psychodynamic therapy, both in post-treatment and 6-month follow-up. The disparity between CBT and supportive therapy was not statistically important in terms of post-treatment or 6-month follow-up clinical response, though those undergoing CBT were more likely to receive therapeutic response than those undergoing supportive therapy. CBT has also demonstrated a greater decrease in post-treatment anxiety and depressive symptoms and 6-month follow-up anxiety than positive therapy. Hunot et al. found mixed outcomes between CT and BT; CT was more likely to result in clinical response, and was more effective in reducing symptoms of depression than BT, but anxiety symptoms were not significantly different. While the most widely cited meta-analysis on care effects for GAD was conducted by Gould, Otto, Pollack, and Yap (1997), Mitte (2005b) published a more comprehensive meta-analysis, involving 65 trials. She found supp-port for CBT 's controlled absolute efficacy in reducing anxiety and depression symptoms and improving quality of life, but did not specifically identify which techniques were considered under CBT's rubric. Many of the patients that dropped out were excluded from the analyses, so the effect sizes reported may have overestimated the actual effects. When analyzing the direct comparisons between CBT and pharmacotherapy, Mitte found that CBT exhibited superiority over pharmacotherapy. However, that effect disappeared when the study population was modified in the sensitivity analyzes. It was therefore decided that CBT would be at least as effective as pharmacotherapy. Overall,

Mitte concluded that the relative effectiveness of CBT and pharmacotherapy remains doubtful, but that CBT appears to be tolerated better than pharmacotherapy. She also noted there had been a high influence of unique CBT treatment factors and a low effect of typical pharmacotherapy influences.

Eating Disorders
Bulimia Nervosa

With at least two meta-analyzes (Whittal, Agras, & Gould, 1999; Lewandowski, Gebing, Anthony, & O'Brien, 1997) and one review (Shapiro et al., 2007) published to date, Bulimia nervosa (BN) has received the greatest attention in the treatment outcome literature on eating disorders. The most recent, thorough, and systematic analysis (including 37 RCTs) was performed by Shapiro et al.; hence only their findings are published. They found good supporting proof of CBT 's total effectiveness, and clear evidence of the significance of CBT 's cognitive aspect in achieving favorable outcomes. They found that CT was superior to supporting only certain measures, and only components of behavioral therapy, ERP, and self-monitoring were superior to nutritional counseling alone, supportive – expressive therapy. However, at 18-month follow-up on certain measures exercise therapy was superior to CBT. When augmenting CBT with ERP, they find no signs of added value. Interpersonal therapy (IPT) and CBT were found to be equal to each other and more effective than waiting-list control in terms of decreases on binged days, psychological characteristics of BN, disinhibition, and restraint when given in a group format. However, a significantly higher probability of remission and greater decreases in vomiting and restraint than individually administered IPT was associated with individually administered CBT. Based on a range of findings, with a variety of drugs being used and outcome measures being examined, Shapiro et al . concluded that preliminary evidence exists for incremental psychotherapy efficacy combined with BN medication.

Hay, Bacaltchuk, and Stefano (2004) reviewed BN, binge — eating disorder (BED) and eating disorder not otherwise defined (EDNOS) psychotherapy literature. For continuous variable outcome data, they calculated relative risks for binary outcome data and standardized mean differences for. Forty RCTs were included in the effects analysis for BN, which investigated the effectiveness of CBT, CBT specifically tailored for bulimia nervosa (CBT-BN), IPT, hypno-behavioral therapy, supportive psychotherapy, and self-control. Researchers observed that all psychotherapies showed total effectiveness relative to waiting-list monitoring on measures of bulimic symptoms and abstinence levels at post-treatment. CBT showed significantly greater improvements in binge-eating abstinence rates than other psychotherapies but not other symptoms of bulimia and psychiatry. Insufficient data were available to compare guided CBT with self-help CBT, and there were no improvements in CBT with CBT comparisons supplemented by ERP or CBT versus "dismantled" CBT. Hay et al . found that CBT-BN was associated with significantly greater improvements in bulimic symptoms and binge-eating rates of abstinence compared to other psychotherapies, but not a greater reduction in scores of depression. The authors concluded that their findings support the effectiveness of CBT, especially that of CBT-BN for BN. They also claimed that other psychotherapies have been effective in the longer term , particularly IPT, and that highly structured self-help CBT is promising, though less so without guidance, and the results are inconclusive specifically with respect to BN. Finally, they deduced that CBT plus ERP alone does not exhibit incremental value above and beyond CBT.

Binge Eating Disorder

While the Hay et al. (2004) analysis included BED, analyzes were conducted as a group on BN, BED, and EDNOS, and not as a distinct condition for BN. Brownley, Berkman, Sedway, Lohr, and Bulik (2007) published a comprehensive analysis of 26 RCTs and, however, discussed treatment effectiveness only for BED. One of the trials they examined reported CBT 's regulated total effectiveness in terms of decreased binged days, body mass index (BMI), disinhibition, nausea , fatigue, self-esteem, and improved chances of abstinence from waiting-list monitors during care. They registered marginal change in weight from baseline to follow-up though. Another research analyzed by Brownley et al . found similar effectiveness in terms of decreasing the number of days binged (at post-treatment and 4-month follow-up) between group CBT and group IPT, although no therapy substantially decreased the BMI. In all groups, frequency of sickness and depression levels were decreased similarly at 12-month follow-up, and rates of abstinence and dropout did not vary among groups. The latter study further found that CBT has resulted in significant gains at all-time rates in the ratings for Eating Disorders Test Restraint. Brownley et al. have observed that a combination of CBT and treatment could boost both eating and weight loss outcomes, but they did not decide which treatments would deliver the most beneficial outcomes. They noted that with both CBT and drug trials the majority of experiments reported pronounced dropout. Bowers and Andersen (2007) concluded that research confirms the effectiveness of CBT in tandem with drugs, but guidelines for treatment can not be made due to shortcomings in the current literature.

The Nervous Anorexia

Bulik, Berkman, Brownley, Sedway, and Lohr (2007) conducted a systematic review of 19 RCTs on the anorexia nervosa (AN) treatment efficacy. They noticed significant gaps in the foundation of literature, and claimed it was inadequate and unpredictable. Despite these limitations, they found tentative supporting evidence for CBT in reducing the risk of relapse for adults after restored weight. Just one study recorded long-term results in which a mixture of CBT and BT resulted in larger changes than those for a placebo group on some steps, but not others, at 12-month follow-up. In the severely underweight community, they find no advantage of CBT over IPT and unspecified supportive clinical intervention. For one research, CBT contributed to decreased risk of relapse and improved positive effects relative to dietary therapy. However, a significant number of trials that reported promising outcomes involved patients who also took antidepressant drugs. That said, Bulik et al. believed that treatment was ineffective for individuals with AN as treatment was associated with high mortality levels and was not correlated with major weight changes or psychological features of AN. Bowers and Andersen (2007) agreed with Bulik et al . (2007) and reported that no data existed to justify the use of antidepressants before and during hospitalization.

Other Causes

Psychophrenia

Schizophrenia psychotherapy is used as an adjunctive pharmacotherapy procedure to improve the control of depressive effects and encourage conformity with the drug. Zimmermann, Favrod, Trieu and Pomini (2005) included 14 studies on positive psychotic symptoms (e.g., hallucinations and delusions) in schizophrenia spectrum disorders in their examination of the treatment outcomes. Overall, CBT showed promising moderate positive effects compared to other adjunctive measures (i.e., standard treatment, waiting list, supportive psychotherapy, and recreation). Additionally, these results marginally improved at early follow-up (3 to 12 months) and were sustained at longer-term follow-up (more than 12 months). However, Zimmermann et al. noted that they were not always blinded, although the experiments used in their analysis were monitored. When they only analyzed the blinded trials, the effect size at post-treatment decreased from 0.37 to 0.29. Further analysis revealed that in comparison with the waiting list, the effects of CBT were greater than in comparison with supportive psychotherapy or treatment as usual. In an acute psychotic episode, CBT has also shown greater effectiveness for patients than for those stabilized chronic patients with enduring psychotic symptoms.

Pilling et al . (2002) carried out a meta-analysis of 18 family therapy and eight CBT trials on data from RCTs. They included a range of strategies under the CBT rubric including challenging and testing key beliefs, modifying dysfunctional beliefs, enhancing coping skills, monitoring the environment and emotion, and psycho-education. They compared family therapy and CBT to either standard care or other treatments, but not directly with one another, depending on the availability of comparison interventions. They found a clear and positive effect on continuous mental-state measures for CBT up to 9 months post-treatment. Although they did not find evidence of increased efficacy of CBT during treatment, CBT showed superiority over all other treatments in terms of significant mental-state improvements during treatment and up to 18 months after treatment. CBT also had a lower attrition rate than standard care and some evidence of improved global post-treatment functioning, but not positive effects on prevention of recurrence or readmission during or after treatment.

Rector and Beck (2001) conducted a meta-analysis for seven RCTs on treatment outcome data that tested the efficacy of CBT for schizophrenia. They found that CBT resulted in large effect sizes, beyond and beyond routine care, on measures of both positive and negative psychotic symptoms. Both groups showed gain retention at a 6-month follow-up, and CBT showed a greater reduction in negative symptoms compared to routine care. CBT showed continued gains on measures of overall symptomatology at 9-month follow-up. CBT also saw greater improvement in both positive and depressive effects associated with compassionate treatment. Gould, Mueser, Bolton, Mays, and Goff (2001) performed a meta-analysis of seven randomized trials and found a fairly significant positive impact size for improvements in depressive symptoms from pre-to post-treatment, which improved therapeutic benefits at 6-month follow-up time.

Marital affliction

Dunn and Schwebel (1995) investigated the effectiveness of cognitive-behavioral marital therapy (CBMT; see Wood, Crane, Schaalje, & Law [2005] for a meta-analysis of marital behavioral therapy [BMT] and marital emotion-focused therapy) for marital distress. Treatments were described as CBMT because they included both therapeutic strategies and an emphasis on "overt efforts to recognise and alter the ill-adaptive cognitions of partners regarding themselves, their partners or the relationship." They observed substantial results at post-treatment and follow-up (1 to 48 months post-treatment) with improvements in behaviour with CBMT, BMT, and interpersonally directed marital therapy (IOMT), but no major variations between treatment modalities. Only CBMT provided a substantial managed effect size on post-treatment relationship-related cognitions, although the effect sizes for BMT and CBMT did not vary substantially, and there were no major follow-up effects either. The effect of post-treatment was investigated for each treatment modality only by one test; substantial post-treatment treatment effects were recorded, and the long-term effects were not substantial, although they were documented only for the IOMT test. All three treatment approaches resulted in significant controlled effect sizes on overall relationship measures and their quality. Post-hoc analyses revealed that IOMT was substantially more successful than BMT and CBMT in bringing about improvement in relationship and consistency of relationships, but this dominance was attenuated at follow-up, as all three methods varied greatly from each other, but not from each other.

Wrath and violent offences

Beck and Fernandez (1998) performed the first meta-analysis of 50 studies in the literature on anger management that directly analyzed CBT, described as a combination of different therapies which may involve mediation, cognitive adjustment, problem solving, and stress inoculation. They reported that CBT was associated with relatively large controlled size of the effect, and that patients with CBT did better than 76 percent of untreated patients on anger reduction. The bulk of the topics used in their study were in violent offender systems. It has not reported any long-term results.

Landenberger and Lipsey (2005) reviewed several meta-analyzes with 58 experimental and quasi-experimental studies and concluded that the effectiveness of CBT for recurrence of violent offenders has been established, but not which CBT variants are most effective or for which offenders. In particular, they found a 25 percent decrease in recurrence rates for the treated group in the 12-month post-treatment compared to the untreated group. They failed to find a difference in effectiveness for different brand-name CBT programs or generic forms of CBT, when they accounted for variables such as high-risk offenders and implementation of high-quality treatments. Both factors have been correlated separately with stronger decreases of recidivism.

Sexual Offending

Psychological and biological therapies for sex criminals published in five languages is reviewed by Lösel and Schmucker (2005). They calculated odds ratios on data from 69 varied research design studies and found that offenders treated with CBT had a 37 percent lower rate of sexual recurrence over an average follow-up period of more than 5 years, and similar rates for violent and general recurrence to controls. Physical treatments had greater effects in terms of relative efficacy than the psychosocial interventions. Specifically, the effect of surgical castration was the greatest, followed by hormonal treatment, CBT, and BT. The latter two were the only psychosocial treatments found to significantly affect sexual recurrence. However, Lösel and Schmucker noted that the difference in effect size between physical and psychosocial treatments has been partially confused by variables of methodology and offender. Specifically, the control groups often refused castration or were not accepted by expert consensus for surgery; thus, they differed markedly from the highly selected and motivated group that opted for surgery voluntarily. Given this consideration, the authors concluded that, in any event, the individuals in the treatment group were probably less likely to reoffend than those in the control group, and that these results could not be found in a truly randomized clinical trial. Due to the aforementioned confounds in the findings and the ethical, legal and medical implications of surgical castration, Lösel and Schmucker designated CBT and hormonal treatments as the most promising treatment options. The particular CBT components have not been identified. Comparisons between group and individual treatments did not yield significantly different results, and only interventions specifically designed for sex offenders had a significant effect; in fact, others showed negative results. Lastly, there were no significant outcome differences between the randomized designs and other research designs. Hanson et al . (2002) performed a similar analysis to the one of Lösel and Schmucker (2005), except that in 43 trials they measured risk ratios and concentrated exclusively on psychiatric therapies. Overall, they found a small advantage in terms of sexual and general recidivism rates for the treated offenders compared with the untreated offenders (over an average follow-up period of 46 months). Treatments employed before 1980 did not show much of an effect on recurrence rates, while current treatments, such as CBT and systemic treatment, were associated with reductions in sexual and general recurrence. Hall (1995) conducted a smaller meta-analysis of just 12 studies and also found a small overall effect size by computing Pearson product—moment correlations for treated versus untreated sex offenders. The findings of Hall differed somewhat from those of Solel and Schmucker (2005) in that they found hormonal treatments and CBT (not defined) to be approximately equally effective in reducing rates of recurrence and significantly more effective than behavioral treatments (average follow-up period of 6.85 years).

Chronic malaise

A meta-analysis of 25 chronic pain studies, excluding headache, was conducted by Morley, Eccleston, and Williams (1999). Outcomes related to pain experience, mood/affect, cognitive coping and assessment, pain behaviour, biology / physical fitness, functioning of social roles, use of health care system and other measures. They classified CBT-based therapies as:

(1) CBT, focusing primarily on changing cognitive activity to bring about changes in behaviour, thinking and emotion;

(2) and the BT; and

(3) Returns on biofeed.

CBT-based treatments were equivalent in all respects to waiting-list restraints, with the exception of pain coping expression. The reported effect sizes were larger for CBT than for BT in all domains except mood/affect, negative cognitive coping and appraisal, and behavioral activity, although the different treatments were not directly compared with each other. Interestingly, biofeedback showed large effect sizes for several domains and was superior to both CBT and BT in pain experience, expression of mood/affect, expression of behavior and functioning of social roles. Morley et al . noted that BT and biofeedback trials were smaller than purely CBT trials. CBT was also advantageous in terms of decreased stress perception and expression relative to a heterogeneous group of other therapeutic therapies, and improved constructive reinforcement but not for other realms. Long term results have not been reported.

Disorders affecting personality

No summary or meta-analytic analysis of the literature on personality disorders was done on the treatment outcome. However, some recent RCTs linked to borderline personality disorder (BPD) have been reported and has gained the greater interest in science. Linehan et al . (2006) and Bohus et al . (2004) examined the effectiveness of dialectical behavioral therapy (DBT; Linehan, 1993), a form of CBT specifically developed for treating BPD. Bohus et al . (2004) observed that in a study of female inpatients 1-month after discharge, DBT resulted in some substantial beneficial decreases and changes. The also had greater clinical improvements on all but two outcome measures compared with the waiting-list controls. Linehan et al . (2006) found equally promising results; in terms of improvements in many scientifically significant effects, DBT has proven preferable to outpatient care.

Also with respect to BPD, Davidson et al . (2006) found no significant differences between a CBT plus treatment group as usual and a treatment group as usual (only) with 12- or 24-month follow-up, but the results favored the former group with 1- and 2-year follow-ups. Although though the research by Brown, Newman, Charles-worth, Christophe, and Beck (2004) was a smaller, unregulated experiment, they observed that CT for BPD was correlated with substantial changes to both post-treatment and 6-month follow-up outcomes. Giesen-Bloo et al . (2006) also found that significantly more patients receiving Young's schema-focused CT (SFCT; Young, Klosko, & Weishaar, 2003) recovered or showed more reliable clinical improvements in measurements of BPD severity, psycho-pathological dysfunction, and quality of life than those receiving psychodynamic transfer-focused psychotherapy (TFP) over a period of 3 years. The TFP group has always reported a higher turnover rate. Finally, Svartberg, Stiles, and Seltzer (2004) observed that on all tests before and after diagnosis, short-term complex psychotherapy and CT provided similarly important benefits to patient. The only significant difference between groups at post-treatment was a change in symptom distress that favored the dynamic group of psychotherapy.

Substance Use Disorders

CBT 's treatment effectiveness has yet to be meta-analysed in the areas of substance use disorders, sleep disorders and somatoform disorders. Review papers for all three disorders do exist, however. Morgenstern and McKay (2007) have recently found consistent empirical support for motivational interviewing, behavioral couple treatment, CBT (i.e., cognitive or behavioral coping skills geared towards substance dependence disorders), and 12-step substance use treatment. They concluded that these interventions had specific effects but found none of them superior to the others, although motivational interviewing produced equivalent results with fewer sessions. A review of the literature recently published in the Cochrane Library was conducted by Denis, Lavie, Fatseas, and Auriacombe (2007).

Because of their heterogeneity, they chose to review six cannabis use treatment studies, rather than meta-analyze them. No definite inference was apparent, but they concluded that psychotherapies in ambulatory conditions, based on poor reported abstinence levels, do not treat cannabis dependency effectively. Hesse (2004) conducted a focused study on the comparative effects of antidepressants and antidepressants in combination with psychotherapy (CBT or manualized, broadly focused counseling) in the treatment of depressive symptoms in persons with comorbid drug or alcohol dependence. They found no significant ben-efit for substance-dependent suicidal patients in combined therapy. Indeed, they found that CBT combined with antidepressants did not reveal any significant effect, and that manualized counseling combined with antidepressants resulted in a smaller effect size than that for medications alone. How-ever, Hesse has determined that the combination may be useful to individuals who don't experience a single treatment success. Long-term results for any of those studies have not been reported.

Disorders Somatoform

Somatoform diseases is the focus of two reports or more. In the diagnosis of hypochondriasis, body dysmorphic disorder (BDD), and undifferentiated somato-form conditions, Looper and Kirmayer (2002) reviewed evidence for CBT. They calculated the possible effect sizes for RCTs and found positive results in treating hypo-chondriasis, BDD, medically unexplained symptoms and functional somatic syndromes for the efficacy of individual CBTs. Researchers also provided supporting evidence for group CBT 's efficacy in treating BDD and somatisation dysfunction. Long term disorder and study results differed. Mai (2004) reviewed somatization disorder etiology, prevalence, diagnosis , and treatment, and found that while somatization disorder is common, few patients seek treatment for mental health. Although CBT appears to be the most effective treatment, some patients may find both antidepressants and supportive therapy effective.

Difficulties in Sleep

Wang, Wang, and Tsai (2005) published a comprehensive literature review on CBT 's efficacy for chronic primary insomnia (PI). They focused exclusively on studies that included adult participants, citing the fact that the mechanism which maintains insomnia in older populations is different because circadian rhythms change with age. They analyzed seven RCTs and concluded that CBT achieved statistically meaningful improvements on outcomes such as increased sleep duration, sleep onset delay, waking after sleep onset, and decreased use of sleep medicine compared with placebo or waiting list. CBT also outperformed less systematic therapies, such as pressure management, calming therapy, and counseling. One research showed that, in tandem with pharmacotherapy, CBT and CBT outperformed pharmacotherapy alone, although there were no major variations in outcomes between CBT and the tandem. The positive benefits of CBT lasted over time (depending on the research, 3 months to 2 years), while those with pharmacotherapy were more time-limited. Wang et al. acknowledged that CBT components differed across trials, leading to challenges in analyzing results. There was common incorporation of behavioral techniques such as stimulus control and sleep hygiene education, but other components, such as relaxation training, differed.

Edinger and Means (2005) have looked at CBT 's usefulness in handling PI. However, they studied only four RCTs not unique to a single age group, and included two of the same studies as Wang et al. Montgomery and Dennis (2003, 2004) reviewed the outcome literature of CBT approaches to increase the consistency, duration, and productivity of sleep in adults aged 60 and over. They found that CBT yielded a mild effect, best proven for insomnia in sleep maintenance. Because of the lack of data to date, they were unable to make conclusive statements about the effectiveness of bright light and exercise for that population. They also suggested that CBT booster sessions could enhance the long-term management of gains.

CHAPTER SIX

Anger Management

If you're saying you're or know someone who's having an anger problem, or you're simply inquisitive, you might wonder-what's anger management? The term is quite coolly thrown around, but it is really a genuine therapy that can help individuals regulate their serious feelings, particularly rage and intense. Many behavioral experts will describe the management of anger as the way the rage is viewed and managed. Anything is not only done once. When you have a problem with frustration, for whatever is left of your life you will be obliged to deal with the issue. If left unchecked, it may end up generating a not insignificant rundown of financial, physical, emotional and enthusiastic problems.

The primary piece of anger management is to identify the problem of rage that you or your adored one may have. Occasionally the vast majority get angry; anger is a natural, strong feeling. When anyone baffles you, or you feel like you have little control except a terrible situation or that you are being manipulated, it is incredibly natural to feel angry. A great many people are furnished in ways that are useful and solid to handle the rage. Individuals requiring anger management may have a difficulty understanding how to respond to their rage feelings. We let it turn into something wild, constantly undermining or harming themselves or others, as opposed to treating it fittingly. Learning what anger management is will help you feel the need for it. You can have a few problems if you have difficulty managing how you feel, particularly when you're angry. In the off chance, you find yourself unable to get over anything or something bad that's been done to you, or you have a propensity to blow up relatively minor problems into huge issues, you may have an anger problem. Whenever you are physically or mentally abusive or crippling, you know you need some help with anger-management programs. Additionally, individuals who have anger management problems can have difficult time sustaining stable ties. There is a reasonable possibility of you not necessarily treating individuals well or fairly if you have a rage problem. Numerous individuals who have any significant rage difficulty will separate individuals from their loved ones.

Individuals can ignore you and your desire to take part in gatherings, conflicts, or wars. Investigate your life and wonder how anger will influence it. Off chance, you'd like to add more valuable contacts and meaningful experiences into your life, but you can't do it because you're always upset, now's the best time to get some anger management for yourself.

There is a wide variety of approaches to taking advantage of care options. You can try doing it all by yourself; use books and other written, specialized, and visual materials. Look for something that discusses what anger management is, and how you can make it work. You can read what specialists have written in the field of emotional well-being, visit blogs, and sign up on the web for bulletins and other info. Teaching yourself about rage and how it affects you is an amazing initial step towards tackling the problem. A good idea is to get assistance from an expert consultant or advocate. You can think about what makes you angry, how you're going to react and how you'd rather proceed.

A specialist will get some details about your history, particularly how you may have been a tyke, how you were born, and how you were exposed as a kid to a significant measure of untamed frustration. This affects the present enthusiastic and mental wellbeing greatly. Your expert will show you amazing strategies for handling frustration and help you track how you're getting along with specific programs and tools. Another perfect way to coping with your frustration is by caregiving classes. Talking with those with anger problems is an exceptional approach. Talking with those with anger issues is an incredible approach to understanding what anger management is and how to do it for your own good. You'll be able to share your own stories and listen to other people's stories. Many things may sound well known to you, and you're going to have the ability to find solace in the way you're not the only one. You'll also know some amazing anger management pitfalls and you can even share some that you might call your own.

Recognize the problem if you or someone you meet is having enthusiastic problems that result from rage issues. When you know that something needs to be achieved with a common end goal to understand a sound and gainful life, you do not have the opportunity to improve. Seek not to ignore the question of frustration that can sneak. Start by teaching yourself what anger management is, so you can choose the tools that function best in your life. Anger is a sensation kids and grown-ups alike witness. If something or someone interferes in an antagonistic way with a human, it may make them feel angry. Anger is a common reaction to an event like this.

Anger may be graded as a mellow aggravation or extraordinary aggravation. Anger may cause a man to end up maddened or even violent, depending on the person, the condition and their feelings. Individuals who are frustrated act in a number of ways. Others lash out, or turn out to be guarded to a great degree. Many people prefer to hush up about their resentment, suppressing their negative feelings and hurt. While a few individuals get to be heedless and even cruel, in case it is not controlled, rage can be a horrendously hurtful feeling. Controlling rage is seen as controlling frustration. A dilemma is a primary move to managing frustration problems it must admit. However, a lot of people have serious rage problems but cannot see it. Everything really happens to set a man off and make them angry. People who have trouble listening to their frustration and tolerating responsibility with regard to their actions frequently play the normal pettiness. We encounter problems close to their problem when they see the situation. Everything, or anyone, is constantly at fault. Their rage attacks are continuously being blamed for something else. Such individuals could really use a couple of anger management lessons. Then again they have to consider their actions and responses for what they are, rage. Numerous individuals with anger issues find it frustrating when it is advised to control frustration. Unable to understand their issue prevents them from finding the assistance they need. In the off chance of a man heading down a road where they are continually angry and moving in, that can cause serious problems in the long run. Without anger management this person is likely to experience tragedy, loss of family, loss of occupation and loss that they may call their own character. It's important to reassure the individual with anger problems, anger management isn't intended to be a discipline but instead to help them get a superior personal satisfaction.

The purpose of anger management is to bail out the individual's problems, bail them out and make sense of why they turn out to be so angry. This also instructs the person not to be oppressed by its emotions, its anger. The aim of anger management is to advise individual procedures to prevent them from having angry too much or for a long time. There is a broad variety of strategies for handling frustration. Projects are made particularly to help people with anger issues. Separate these programs to discuss distinctive individuals, infants, teens, grown-ups, couples and families. Such anger-management programs are set up to demonstrate or help people chip away from their anger. Through anger management, it is important to teach people strategies for sorting out their problems and managing their anger.

Learning about Feelings and Anger

There are actually individuals who are going to classes on self-development to find out about inclusion and attestation. Self-development is a process a person conducts to better his or her life. Quite a few people from a variety of points of view are seeking to improve their lives. They learn through the use of various open tools to attain inner peace. In any case, there are a number of people who don't accomplish goals even in the wake of making an attempt to accomplish them. We are preoccupied with fear. You should conquer tension on the off chance you need to achieve self-growth. It has been pointed out that multiple people struggle with anxiety. In the off chance individuals have the potential to properly use meditation, then they find themselves capable of managing tension. Under what way does meditation allow you to cope with stress? It lets you discover your identity inside. You understand yourself better. By it your talents for self-advancement are pushed forward. Just constructive considerations should be thought about on the basis that you should have learned to the best way to handle negative considerations. We get pulled up and makes us irritated because we don't really know.

We're not able to tackle the daily challenges of life with the fearlessness. Because we aren't able to think vigorously to tackle life's challenges day by day, we get stuck. Along these lines, larger portions of anxiety-finding people are people who consider of negative thoughts. We do not see themselves losing a wonderful thing in life. You should work out how to take it easy and make your brain relax. Confirm that you need to be in life you should be. To remain strong, use reflexion to ruminate good things and use activities. To remain strong, training is a ruminate of good items and practices of use. Practicing is a ruminating tool. Moving on a fitness and wellness routine will boost your physical, moral and inner feelings. It would improve your cerebral functioning. As a consequence, your brain will unwind you will not be concentrated in any way. Once you exercise the body, bite the dust cells will be put together with new ones.

Once you make new cells in your body, your shot of living would have grown further. There are ways to keep the brain responsive so you can stay away from anxiety. One way you can make use of this is by writing to complement the reflection. Compose a log, or account of your life. It will allow you aware of your intellectual energy along certain lines to relieve your anxiety. Given the fact that documenting your past life, you'll be able to imagine your future because you'll figure out what you have to do with your life. Recording a diary will help you explore your brain and concoct new thoughts. When you've decided what you need, log the goals you're going to use to accomplish what you need. This will allow your psyche to have a fair excuse to log the goals.

You will carry out valuable changes by contemplation which will give you a new look. Learn the most knowledgeable method for managing your rage, particularly when you're bothered by someone. You are vulnerable to being concentrated on in case you start to get angry. Settle down on wanting to let that frustration out. The word anxiety is a development usually of the present day. The terms for indignation are as old as time, whatever it may be. "Cain rose in wrath," it says in Genesis. Anger has always been showing to us from the very beginning of history that it cuts both directions. The antique Chinese said, "You are constantly smoldering more than he by the flame you light for your opponent." We call that flaming fear. Which are the reasons for its anger? One natural way of taking a gander at it considers indignation to be an after-effect of disconcerted impulses... Desires coming out of our inner self. "You" did not fulfill your promise to "me," or let me down, or hurt me, or offended me, or forgot to consider me, or bamboozled me, or cut me off in action, or said or did a heap of imaginable stuff, and now "I" am furious about "you." The doubly annoying thing about anger, is that "you," the victim of my anger in this case, might be totally uninformed of my anger, or in the event of your wrath,

You could not even give a second thought, on the other hand. I may fuminate weeks after whatever slight you've done, my head hurts, my stomach is burning, and my heart pounds at the chance I think I need to see you again. However, I am most definitely doubly offended in case you have overlooked feeling sorry. Why can we overcome anxiety and anger? At source. We will reverse our story and tell you're the wrathful one. That is what makes you the source. You may now speculate that the situation is brought on by whoever did the thing that made you angry, but the rage is your reaction, and yours alone. Their behavior may have been dangerous, idiotic, or unwise, or by some stretch of the imagination, it may have nothing to do with you. They act, or forget to act, and it is done. Until you angrily react, and things start up again. If you strike back in your rage, and allow your rage to turn into violence, you start a whole new cycle that can continue through time. Just check out the planet to see people suffering intense fear and misery, from a crazy wave of frustration a thousand years ago.

Anger may also have its roots in fear or sorrow. If you've ever been upset with your kid over any heedless behaviour, your frustration is the way you show your heightened trepidation. You're frenzied about the fact that seeing him in danger just upsets you to death. The death of a life partner or one loved brings a peculiar rage from surrender feelings, which are a typical piece of misery. Both these kinds of rage are the product of your suffering fear and the pain it will offer you. This kind of anxiety you feel will make you feel numb, but it will pass in the long run. How to control the frustration and push? Whatever the reasoning, let out the rage. Playing, beating a punching bag, or pounding your couch with a Nerf bat all the effort out of your frame to get adrenaline. At that point you need to quickly inhale deeply and use unwinding techniques to cool off. Although it doesn't value "contain" anger, raving and hollering just elevates difficult feelings. Find some soothing solution to discharge your pain, and at a more fitting time you can handle the issue smoothly. To neglect to respond, settle on a cognizant option.

Rage might sound like a pre-programmed message but you might be prepared not to respond like that. In case you have wishes unfulfilled, stop believing what will never happen. A lot of rage when our accomplices fail to live up to our expectations comes because we can't accept them as they seem to be. This can take a lot of practice, so let little begin. Nevertheless, in case you discover that you can roll out an improvement in a blaze, don't be surprised, because individuals who roll out you will appreciate improvement right next to you. Practice, work out, baby. Extraordinary piano players have never stopped performing scales. Rehearsing meditation and absolution will save you from much fear and frustration in your future, for the rest of your life. Today is the start of an amazing day.

Learning about Helpful and Unhelpful Ways

When you feel like a liquid magma fountain swirling in your head, take a moment to get your calm back and remember that there are no less than three solutions to managing your rage: you can either express your frustration, smother it, or cool off. Whatever you pick, it's going to help you control your rage. Communicate your indignation-Indeed, go ahead and blast! Relinquish the smoldering feeling inside your mid-section, and let it be hard and fast. Be that as it may, one thing you need to know-yes, you may express your frustration but don't give it a chance to escape control and transform into a destructive force to damage both your frustration's wellspring and yourself too. Rage is the tacit portion of man's barrier to avert risk, to guarantee our survival when assaulted. Our heart rate, pulse, vitality hormones, and adrenaline all go up when we're angry, making us visibly and physically more grounded to fight off a threat.

However, of course, anger has a few degrees. You can't compare an opponent who just wants to wound your heart with the same degree of contempt as a guy who just made you incredibly angry. Social norms, laws and skills in practical judgment guide us to manage our rage based on the severity of the dangers we face. We can not express karate blows against any person who ultimately chafes us or disturbs us. Be that as it may, yes, even now you can communicate your compelling feelings to someone who is basically irritating you. Be vigilant though not to insult him excessively; don't call him awful names for incidence. Clearly tell the person in his face that his actions irritates you, and makes you feel uncomfortable.

Smothering your rage-Another way of managing your boiling over your feeling is to stifle it, turn it over, or approach your boiling over your feeling is to stifle it, turn it or sidetrack it. In the off chance you feel it's not yet time to express your frustration, you may want to stop it, stop pondering it or try doing something constructive. In any case, the risk here is that you will blast the dormant emotions inside you, which can lead to issues of well-being such as hypertension, depression or hypertension. Unreleased rage may also cause different problems, such as hitting back at the apparent rival in a roundabout way, or criticizing individuals even without legitimation. Silence yourself-Calming yourself is the best option among the three methods to regulate frustration, without confusion. You regulate your external actions as well as your emotions as you do so, thereby forestalling both physical showdowns-which will eventually damage you-and internal conflicts that could damage your well-being. While this is the best option, this is nevertheless the hardest to do. Yet, mental health and the right attitude will certainly help you to control your rage in the best possible way, in addition to good support from minding friends or relatives.

Rage support management is particularly useful because it is extraordinarily difficult to handle or alter repetitive behaviour. It will be safer for people to build and sustain progression if a care organization or another person actually checks them and takes care of them. This can also be done by a mixed bag of means, maybe by expert sources, boost workplaces, and friends and relatives. Classes on anger management are accessible to government or company agencies, private foundations, head honchos or relatives. In view of the genuine problem or kind of frustration that you have, these classes will provide support and projects. The amount of time, topics, and class activities can differ, depending on your particular issues and needs. Furthermore, there are tasks and assessments that will gage your development.

Some kind of technique for helping control the rage is a test of your success. This kind of technique of anger help management is strong, especially in a class in which other "furious" people likewise enter. In case you believe you can deal openly with anger problems, self-study is another useful technique for handling anger support. You will have the potential to communicate more and more easily with your own issues and mentalities, in comparison to joining a group. An advocate and teacher's role is still imperative for self-study, so the position can be assumed by an experienced professor, professional or a steady relative. When issues vary and opinions among furious individuals can be more subjective in nature, self-study is a good opportunity to transcend these. Additionally, rage support management tools are available to support you adjust and better sense your feelings. There are sound apps that you can listen to for self-improvement. Relaxing music tends to calm emotions and faculties, Stress balls and games act as a yield for frustration, whereas a generally friendly atmosphere is extremely favorable to relieve anxiety. Find out how to differentiate materials that will help you deal with your frustration and rising tension for sustained development. In case you feel the ill effects of the issue of marginal identity, then the steady fear of other people's relinquishment or control could be extremely well known to you. Moreover, this may be the reason behind why you continue to get frustration and rope out on others, similar to family, friends or partners in the workplace. In case you consider yourself in the above instances, let me remind you that you are not the only one in the light of the fact that with this identity question there are millions all over the world. Perhaps I'd like to send you five strategies that you can quickly and rapidly introduce to avoid the upheavals of your wrath. The original one is the form of breathing and can be combined with statements for better outcomes. If you feel angry at the ensuing occurrence, try to remember STOPING for a brief moment, close your eyes, slowly inhale through your nose, and slowly breathe out through your mouth. Repeat it no less than three times. Via your mouth you can boost the. Repeat it no less than three times. Through insistences you can maximize the smoothing effect of moderate and maximum breaths, which you can tell rationally or loudly. In view of the fact that it goes straight to your intuitive nature this self-talk is highly proficient. A few examples of such attestations are "I'm relaxed," "I'm silent," "I'm silent," or "I'm positive." You can say "I'm calm" when you take in, and "I'm casual" when you breathe out. And the emotions and body reactions are consciously sensed as they shift and transform into more constructive and welcoming ones. You'll be shocked when it turns out that it really easily lives up to expectations. The second method is to hold an individual journal where you can bring all of your external and inner critical experiences into it. Imagine your newspaper as your nearest friend where you may go in difficult times where you don't pass judgment or reproach. Likewise, writing in your own journal will assist you with all the unhelpful thoughts and warning triggers that you constantly express in your head, along with new viewpoints on what is going on with your life by "playing" your life back. The third approach is to seek to find realistic and rational reasons to explain yourself that the other person does not want to desert, punish or harm you.

It is serious, and will allow you to avoid your residual frustration by a significant amount. In the light of previous experiences, marginal individuals continue to offer overstated consequences to the actions and behaviors of others although this is not the case more often than not. Help yourself out and try to discover honestly why the translation is an explosion of rational and valid thought processes. The fourth approach that I may like to leave you with stops the residual frustration behavioral signal by supplanting it with a mental operation. Next sign of marginal frustration by making a mental task supplant it. Next event when you feel upset, I would suggest that you do the breathing exercise first in combination with the confirmations to avoid the propensity of aggressive talk and actions. Then take yourself a few minutes to watch, call, and acknowledge your experiences within.

The Cognitive Aspect of Anger Management

Anger exhorting is a various splendored beast. Ever heard that old AA expression or abbreviation HALT, for example? The abbreviation suggests that we are at progressively genuine danger for falls away from the faith when we are voracious, irate, desolate, or tired. Yearning, dejection, exhaustion, shut head harm, ADD, ADHD, gathering of source, impulse and recovery, misery, pardon and bargain, modified negative examinations, push, our reaction to outward appearances, all can have impact in the energetic experience of anger.

We ought to have anger by chance; it is the vitality we use to deal with issues. In addition, it is likewise a discretionary feeling, generally speaking, taking after another feeling like hurt or disrespect. In any case, if we use anger to legitimize unpleasantness I think we subvert the purpose behind our feelings. The one thing that no other anger the executives program that I am aware of talks about is the speed of the Central Nervous System (CNS). That is 2x as brisk as I can gleam my eyes, which takes 1/tenth second. So you have to have your anger prompting instruments in a spot where they can be checked on quickly.

I likewise prefer to help people in anger exhorting fathom that their inside science or hormones change with each thought they have, and that we as individuals have all things considered around 200 contemplations for every day which change our science toward disturbance and that we ought to be orchestrated to name our sentiments, their force, and to settle on a couple of choices about transforming our sentiments, their force, and to settle on a couple of choices about transforming them significantly more as frequently as could reasonably be expected and a lot speedier than perhaps we presumed we did. Sounds like care, isn't that right? Care, or awareness of what I am feeling joined with significant breathing gives me a viable device to cool off if I am finding a workable pace. Take your heartbeat, and if it is in excess of 100 bangs for every minute, take no under 20 minutes, especially for men, to calm down. Repeat that methodology as much of the time as crucial.

Another gadget that I train for the mindfulness and care some portion of anger controlling in a biofeedback mechanical assembly, called Heartmath, which readies the capacity to deal with the time between heart throbs. At the point when you learn Heartmath, you can feel incredible on enthusiasm, on some random heartbeat. Your heartbeat is actually a piece more slow than your CNS, yet it is an a lot shorter mediation time than a large portion of us are used to. Heartmath is taking into account investigation in the starting late discovered field of neuroradiology, which is the examination of the heart's own tactile framework.

The heart sends a ton of data to the psyche about how we are feeling, generously more than the cerebrum sends to the heart, and the heart's cerebrum is an offshoot and accommodating cerebrum, which is extraordinary brain to use in dealing uneasiness.

Heartmath meets desires for your golf score and your cerebrum wellbeing also. Anger directing including Rational Emotive Behavior Therapy (REBT) or Cognitive Behavioral Therapy (CBT) will incorporate affirmation of modified negative contemplations and discussing them on account of REBT or making a stream diagram of evidence supporting your hot thought and affirmation disavowing your hot thought on account of CBT. By the day's end, mindfulness will be a key piece of the anger-prompting enigma, yet this period of examinations, not just physiology or heartbeat. It is shocking to me that our lifestyle instructs the anguish change so insufficiently. So a large portion of my clients have a presence time of ungreased misfortunes and saw abandonments which influence their capacity to trust, and if their CNS is overwhelmed by the physiology associated with a memory, their body might be moving before they can think about taking a heartbeat.

What is Anger?

Anger is a term for the enthusiastic piece of hostility, as a principal part of the uneasiness reaction in animals whereby an obvious upsetting lift "actuates" a counter reaction which is in like way disturbing and crippling of unpleasantness. Outstandingly delicate sorts of anger are normally delineated as "disdain," "alarm", or "annoying," while "savagery" suggests an incredible degree of anger associated with lost smoothness or control (on account of human conduct). In front line society, anger is viewed as an adolescent or grungy reaction to disappointment, hazard, encroachment, or misfortune. On the other hand, fighting the temptation to freeze, collected, or deciding not to fight back is seen as even more socially acceptable.

This embellishment can achieve wrong expressions of anger, for instance, uncontrolled, savage changes or deceived anger, or, at the other astonishing, repressing sentiments of anger (or lacking them overall) when those feelings would be a fitting reaction to the situation. Likewise, anger that is consistently "smothered" can incite decided merciless examinations or awful dreams, or even physical symptoms like cerebral torments, ulcers, or hypertension.

Anger Side Effects

Anger can upset a couple of passionate prosperity issues. Anger can fuel debilitation. Individuals who are discouraged all things considered don't deal with themselves. They live it up dangerous activities, for instance, an overabundance of drinking, smoking, gorging, risking everything, and not watching their assets. Discouraged individuals have less vitality, diminished desiring, and need more rest. Their work execution will drop and associations will separate.

Various individuals acknowledge that dejection is in all honesty anger turned interior. The reason behind this supposition is on account of various depressives react to push by turning their anger inner as a reaction to physical or mental abuse, or dismissal from people or gatekeeper figures. After a short time, the adjusting instruments find a good pace that they use inappropriately and eccentrically at whatever point they see misfortune or disappointment.

Depressives tend to grow up tolerating that if they are hurt or misused, there are only two choices available, which are self-accuse and foreswearing of fault. One helper effect of the burdensome's refusal of anger is that their relational associations are often hopeless and they don't get the "breaks" that others seem to get. They may not get progressions, social invites or love in light of the fact that truth be told by far most would lean toward not to be around discouraged individuals for any timeframe, both at home and grinding away. Another side effect of anger is that it can fuel obsessions, fears and addictions.

Obsessions and fears rise up out of conditions when, for no good reason or another, we believe we are either losing control of ourselves or our general environment. Anger can likewise fuel hyper tendencies. Various individuals who are not prepared to express their anger let it out in irate activity. Once in a while this development accomplishes a cutoff and results in clinical depression or even bipolar issue. Anger can likewise fan the flares of distrustfulness and bias, even in run of the mill, Anger can likewise fan the flares of distrustfulness and bias, even in common, customary conditions.

Individuals tend to express their anger either idly or forcefully with the basic "flight" reaction, which is restriction and refusal of anger. Forceful lead is associated with the "fight" reaction and the usage of the verbal and physical force of anger to misuse and hurt others.

Reactions of Anger

Anger can be of one of two rule sorts: standoffish anger and forceful anger.

These sorts of anger have some trademark reactions:

Detached Anger

Detached anger can be communicated in going with ways:

1. Covered direct, for instance, storing feelings of disdain that are communicated behind individuals' backs or through insightful tunnels, giving the quiet treatment or under the breath mutterings, keeping up a vital good ways from eye to eye connection, putting individuals down, snitch, obscure protestations, poisonous substance pen letters, taking, and conning.

2. Control, for instance, prompting individuals to hostility and thereafter putting down exonerating, actuating ill will anyway staying centered sidelines, energetic blackmail, incredible melancholy, imagining sickness, assaulting associations, using sexual impelling, using an untouchable to pass on negative feelings, retaining money or resources.

3. Self-fault, for instance, saying 'sorry' over and over, being unreasonably segregating, and inviting input. Benevolence, for instance, being too much valuable, particularly making do with second best, and unpretentiously making tolerant signs anyway dismissing help, or drinking up gratefulness and making all around arranged tunnels where it isn't imminent.

4. Lacking, for instance, setting yourself just as others up for disappointment, picking conflicting individuals to depend on after, being cumbersome, underachieving, sexual weakness, conveying disappointment at unimportant things anyway ignoring authentic ones.

5. Unprejudiced, for instance, treating with complete contempt or sham smiles, looking cool, sitting going to and fro while others deal with things, hosing feelings with substance abuse (to fuse gorging), snoozing, not responding to other's anger, chill, getting a charge out of sexual practices that debilitate suddenness and make objects of individuals, giving unnecessary proportions of time to machines, things or insightful interests, talking about disappointments yet exhibiting no tendency.

6. Fixation direct, for instance, holding on to be unadulterated and clean, making an inclination for constantly checking, over-expending less calories or gorging, mentioning that all occupations are done marvelously.

7. Quibble, for instance, turning you in a crisis, avoiding conflict, not battling back, finding a good pace.

Forceful Anger

The signs of forceful anger are:

1. Incapacitating, for instance, alarming individuals by saying how you could hurt them, their property or their possibilities, fault administering, grip hand shaking, wearing dresses associated with merciless lead, driving on someone's tail, setting on an auto horn, pulverizing gateways.

2. Awful, for instance, physical brutality, verbal abuse, off the mark jokes, breaking an assurance, playing boisterous music, using foul tongue, ignoring individuals' emotions, resolvedly

isolating, blaming, or rebuking individuals for deeds they are known not to have presented, naming others.

3. Perilous, for instance, harming articles, intentionally destroying a connection between two individuals, driving imprudently, drinking unnecessarily.

4. Tormenting, for instance, crippling individuals, distressing, pushing or pushing, using vitality to oppress, hollering, using a compelling auto to drive someone off the road, playing on individuals' inadequacies.

5. Disgracefully blaming, for instance, reviling others for your own specific mistakes, blaming individuals for your own specific emotions, making general charges.

6. Hyper, for instance, talking excessively quick, walking excessively quick, meeting desires a ton of and envisioning that others should fit in, driving excessively quick, careless spending.

7. Gaudy, for instance, parading, conveying questions, not appointing, being a poor disappointment, requiring center of everybody's consideration continually, not tuning in, talking over individuals' heads, anticipating that kiss and make-up meetings should handle issues.

8. Silly, for instance, ignoring other's necessities, not responding to requests help, line ricocheting, 'cutting in' when driving.

9. Malicious, for instance, being over-reformatory, declining to reason and neglect, raising awful memories from an earlier time.

10. Fanciful, for instance, blowing hot and cool, hazardous furies over minor disillusionments, attacking eccentrically, directing order all of a sudden, demanding naughtiness on other just with the end goal of it, using drink and prescriptions that are known not perspective, using irrational conflicts.

Tips on Anger Management

Loosening up

Basic loosening up mechanical assemblies, for instance, significant breathing and loosening up basic loosening up contraptions, for instance, significant breathing and loosening up imagery, can assist cool with offing perturbed suppositions. There are books and courses that can show you loosening up techniques, and once you take in the methodology, you can call upon them in any situation. If you are remembered for a relationship where the two accessories are hot-tempered, it might be a shrewd idea for both of you to take in these frameworks.

Some basic steps you can attempt:

• Inhale significantly, from your stomach; breathing from your midriff won't unwind you. Picture your breath coming up from your "gut."

- Gradually go over a peaceful word or expression, for instance, "unwind," "unwind." Repeat it to yourself while breathing significantly.

- Use imagery; imagine an unwinding information, from either your memory or your imaginative capacity.

- Non-strenuous, moderate yoga-like exercises can unwind your muscles and make you feel a lot calmer. Practice these methodologies consistently. Make sense of how to use them normally when you're in a stressed situation.

Those searching for anger management systems can normally advantage hugely from master intervention and likewise through achieving a perception of this exceptionally amazing inclination. In various families, irate sentiments are dispirited and youngsters grow up dubious and humiliated each time they experience an opposing inclination. In any case, anger can be an exceptionally positive and strong inclination when coordinated precisely and conveyed in a balanced manner. Exactly when endeavoring to see such a competent inclination, it tends to be valuable to understand that anger will customarily be contained a couple of components. These parts might be abstract, mental, and physiological in nature. The scholarly component needs to do with the specific habits of reasoning that the individual is experiencing. From time to time, a principal appreciation that sentiments of exacerbation are both normal and upheld can be exceptionally helpful. The psychological fragment will manage precisely how the individual feels. Despite furious sentiments, the individual might be feeling disheartened, perplexed, or let down. Taking a gander at all of these emotions and the clarifications for them can be exceptionally convincing anger management techniques. The physiological viewpoints will manage the body's physical reaction to irate sentiments. Does the pulse increase? Does the circulatory strain rise? Is there an appearance of adrenaline? Explaining such components can make it plain to the patient precisely why the need to reasonably channel successful feelings is so basic to the particular's general prosperity. The triggers for irate feelings are typically a type of bewildering event.

Additional conditions, for instance, a longstanding and fundamental disappointment can moreover be contributing components. If someone seems to encounter life feeling endlessly irate, this could be a sign of a huge issue that may profit by the fruitful usage of various anger management strategies. Since these issues will, as a general rule originate from a type of instructed lead, new learned practices could supply the necessary fix. Dealing with irate feelings may generally be refined in one of two different ways, expression or camouflage. Sound expression wo exclude upheavals and impacts, anyway, will typically be depicted by cool assessment, lively supplications or certain clarifications.

The individuals who are more allured to smother anger may have an exceptionally problematic time with such a great amount of issues as strong articulation over wrong antagonistic vibe or impassioned, anyway controlled solicitations. Practical anger management systems can help those on the two sides of the range. Any individual who is slanted to furious upheavals can profit by figuring out how to communicate emotions without turning commanding or cruel toward others. Those in the inclination for covering sentiments of anger can find a lot of lightening in figuring out how to impart since a long time back canvassed feelings easing in figuring out how to impart since a long time prior shrouded feelings in sound and helpful manners. Once in a while, the help of a specialist promoter might be required.

A counselor will normally research the persevering's family establishment and youth to pick up an unrivaled perception of the principal purposes behind the issues that the individual presents. Shrewd people can help their youngsters by indicating them fruitful anger management strategies in the midst of youth. Anger is fundamental among youngsters. Disapproving of people can educate both by test and by providing the kid with accommodating contraptions for dealing with these extraordinary feelings. A couple of youngsters may use anger as a way to deal with pick up thought or consolation from people. This can present various issues for concerned moms and fathers. The need to prepare wrong lead must be joined with a consolation that the kid is valued really. While there should be results for furious upheavals, rule on the most ideal approach to more readily communicate these sentiments is a verifiable necessity.

Subsequently, a guardian can every now and again remove various issues and better set up the kid for life in the adult world. Clearly, there can be various different purposes for the wrong impacts of furiousness. The youth might be endeavoring to pick up power or might be searching for a requital or threatening vibe toward another person. Master coordinating nearby the utilization of anger management systems can be exceptionally helpful in dealing with and finding the purposes for a kid's astonishing behavior issues. For youngsters, there are different anger management techniques that might be feasible. The high researcher years can be both irksome and overwhelming. A specific proportion of furious emotions in the midst of the energetic years is both regular and sensible. Figuring out how to sufficiently deal with these emotions is a bit of the common advancement process. In any case, for a couple of young people, anger can escape from control and find a good pace.

Right when this is the circumstance, master exhorting might be all together. A guardian can enable their adolescent to deal with this wrath by keeping the lines of correspondence open. If the teenager feels that they have lost parental regard and remote possibility that the teenager feels that they have lost parental regard and underwriting after a change, this may simply add to the issue. Exploring the wellsprings of nervousness that the energetic might be feeling can be helpful as well. If a fundamental issue is remembered, it may be less requesting to find a reliable plan.

Anger Frequency

How often people get angry certainly varies culturally, but there is little data outside of North American samples in this respect. Work by G started the study of universal forms of rage. Stanley Hall (1899), and Averill (1982) conducted the most detailed work. Between these studies and several subsequent a variety of small sample studies were conducted over the decades. On average, people have reported becoming angry two to three times a week in this research. The results recorded in the analysis by Russian (St. Petersburg) and American (New York) participants from Kassinove et al. (1997) revealed a bimodal spread between samples, with 25 percent recorded rage occurring a few days a week and 33 percent less than once a week (but more than once a month). In anger frequency the Americans were significantly higher than the Russians, as reflected in 11 percent of the former reporting becoming angry once a day or more, whereas this was the case for only 3 percent for the latter. Kassinove et al. did not find any gender differences in the frequency of anger and this is a common finding.

A review of data obtained by the US General Social Survey (Davis & Smith, 1996), available as an electronic database, to further examine the question of anger frequency. When asked 634 men and 817 women, "How many days have you felt angry about someone in the past seven days? "63.4 percent of the sample reported being angry the week before, with 20.3 percent reporting being angry three days or more. No significant gender differences were found, as both males and females were equally likely to say they had felt anger over the past week. Similar to what is routinely found in psychological research regarding aggressive behaviour, age was correlated inversely with anger frequency. If we consider "frequent anger" to get angry three or more days a week, people under the age of 30 were most likely to report this (26.7%), while those over the age of 64 were less likely (9.5%) to report it. The chi-square test was statistically significant across age groups; $\lambda 2(4) = 85.57$, $p < 0.001$. Curiously, the higher salary was correlated with a greater probability of more regular frustration coverage.

Then, if these largely US data are a guide, it would seem reasonable to consider someone who reports becoming angry every day, to be high in anger frequency. But there are significant cultural variations to consider. Episodes of daily anger are quite common in Rome and Naples in the authors' personal experience, whereas getting angry in China is relatively rare. More broadly, it would be fair to assume that a person who experiences two to three times daily being frustrated would be considered elevated in anger level.

Anger Intensity

Rage severity levels are a hallmark feature of psychometric anger such as the State Factor Anger Speech Inventory (STAXI) by Spielberger (1988) and the Novaco Agitation Inventory (NPI) (Novaco, 1983). Higher intensity ratings are assumed to be indicative of greater disturbance, since the ratings are summarized across items. Indeed, the intensity dimension functions as a qualitative discrimination because, by virtue of the intensity of the effect, we partially judge that we are angry, as opposed to being "upset," "bothered" or "annoyed." Without frequency, degree of strength is even more specifically reflective of impairment, as an inherent factor is physiological stimulation. Scientifically it is well known that high enthusiasm interferes with performance, particularly mental processes involved in complex tasks. High-intensity anger, in addition to having cognitive interference effects, leads to impulsive behavior as it overrides inhibitory controls. In an anger episode, people often judge their intensity of anger from their behaviour, though this is more the case for men than for women.

In a review of results from the US General Social Survey (Davis & Smith, 1996), those who reported they had been angry the previous month (N = 1115; 477 males and 638 females) were asked, "How intense would you think your frustration or annoyance was? "And were asked to rate their anger on a 0 to 10 scale. Similar to what was observed for duration, the strength of indignation was inversely correlated with age: $\pi2(4)=24.94$, p<.001. There were variations in strength between genders, however. Women (64.7 percent) were more likely to rate their anger at or above a level of 6 than men (55.1 percent), but this is at variance with the lack of gender differences in many studies. For example, in either the American or Russian samples, Kassinove et al . (1997) found no gender differences in anger intensity.

Trauma groups are prone to suffer rage disorders, and Ehlers et al . (1998) performed a major review in Britain on individuals involved in a motor car crash with regards to post-traumatic stress disorder (PTSD) related to rage severity and class. Immediately after the crash they examined 967 people (521 men and 446 women), and again after three months and one year. No differences between men and women were found at any of the evaluations. Women were as likely as men to send "very angry" or "highly angry" self-ratings, which, when measured, represented 22.1% of men and 25.1% of women at the initial evaluation (A. Ehlers, Personal Contact, 11 and 18 February 1999). Although it has also been observed that women and men feel rage at similar levels of severity, men are more inclined to evaluate anger severity from their actions while women are more inclined to measure anger length while measuring their anger intensity.

Duration

The intensity of the anger can be expected to influence the duration of anger for a number of reasons:

(A) Higher physiological activation acceleration is associated with longer duration of recovery to baseline;

(B) circumstances which cause great anger can intensify and spread as a result of angry behaviour;

(C) High anger arises from matters of significant importance to the victim, and those consequences are likely to continue and not be addressed promptly — this contributes to ruminations on the causative factors that perpetuate and rekindle frustration.

There is significant inter-subjective variation, both within and through trials, in the length of frustration episodes. Early work by Gates (1926) and Melzer (1933) found , for example, average durations of 15–20 minutes. Several research in monograph Averill (1982) find the median period to be around one hour. In the analysis by Kassinove et al. (1997), 39 percent of the US sample and 53 percent of the Russian sample registered a period of anger of 30 minutes or less. Curiously, 31 per cent and 20 per cent of U.S. and Russian samples registered a full day or more of rage, respectively. Similarly, for anger duration of one day or more, Averill (1982) had found a 25 percent endorsement rate. It can not be interpreted straightforwardly when people report anger for such long periods, because it is doubtful that arousal and effect are continuously present throughout the interval. The explanation for this estimation of the length is more likely to be because feelings about the rage event have resurfaced during the day.

Rumination is a troubling feature of reactions to anger. The duration of the anger episode was not assessed in the U.S. General Social Survey (Davis & Smith, 1996), but the survey asked about anger being reactivated through thoughts (N = 943; 415 males, 528 females). Women (17.2 percent) were more likely than men (11.8 percent) to report "very frequently" thinking about the anger situation Š 2(2) = 6.1, p<.05—but there were no differences between genders in the likelihood of thinking about revenge. Revenge feelings diminish dramatically with age.

The prolongation of the excitement of anger has several troubling consequences. First, prolonged anger and its non-expression have a significant effect on blood pressure and this is a substantial factor in essential hypertension. Second, if frustration arousal does not return to normal, there are likely to be "excitation transition" results, whereby the undissipated arousal leads to anticipation from new stimuli and raises the probability of offensive actions (Zillmann & Bryant, 1974). Third, ruminating about incidents of anger interferes with optimum functioning and diminishes positive inputs that strengthen the self.

Mode of Expression

Anger 's behavioral manifestation is the feature with greatest societal import. Most problematically, rage causes emotional as well as physical violence. Verbal abuse includes aggressive , violent, and disrespectful comments whose common denominator is to generate anxiety in the target person. Physical violence, which is an overt action aimed at inflicting injury or destruction, can either be directed at the offending individual or moved to a substitute target. Rage may also inspire "passive" hostility, which in a veiled form is negative action — implied congeniality, intentional emotional coldness, or indifference, with the purpose of inducing pain in the goal. In addition to these forms of harm-intended behaviour, anger can be expressed in constructively minded problem-solving behaviour, or secure ventilation given. Aggressive behaviour, except in the home and in psychiatric and correctional institutions, generally has low base rate. In the data from the US General Social Survey, in response to the question, "Have you yelled or hit something to let your pent-up feelings out? "Relatively few respondents (N = 1114) said yes (7.9%) and males were a little more inclined. The relation was curvilinear with age. Kassinove et al . (1997) found that 11% of the U.S. sample and 8% of the Russian sample either fought or hit the provoking person or hit something or destroyed it. For 38 percent of the Americans (New Yorkers) and 22 percent of the Russians there was yelling and arguing. "Men more often reported fighting or hitting a human. Yet women were more likely to shout and argue "(p. 314). Unfortunately, Kassinove et al. did not cross-tabulate behavioral expression with target person status, but 62% of the U.S. sample and 58% of the Russian sample reported an anger episode involving either someone they knew and liked or someone they loved. And a large proportion of the incidents of rage could have been provocations surrounding relatives or intimates.

Domestic abuse, globally, is a growing societal issue. The estimated 1996 Uk Crime Report for 1995 overall number of cases of domestic abuse was 6.6 million. Nevertheless, the definition of domestic violence used by the Home Office was specific and involved sexual harassment. In the USA, a recent survey jointly sponsored by the National Institute for Justice and the Centers for Disease Control found that in the 12 months preceding the survey, 5.9 million physical assaults were perpetrated against women for a representative sample of 8000 women. This was experienced by intimates by the majority of women (64 percent) who had been victimized by rape, physical assault or stalking since the age of 18.

Similarly, the 1997 Criminal Statistics for England and Wales show that the partners killed 47 percent of the 224 female homicide victims, while their partners killed only 8 percent of the 426 male homicide victims.

Violence victimization has been extensively documented to have a host of adverse consequences for women in the short and long term. It is well recognized that severe difficulties of psychological adjustment, such as PTSD and major depression, are a common consequence for abused women. At least 3.3 million children in the USA are estimated to be at risk of exposure to domestic violence annually. The detrimental effects on a child witnessing violence between parents include trauma and learning to respond to conflict with violent behaviour, each of which has long-term consequences for the psychological adjustment and well-being of a child. While some have questioned the weight that should be given to anger in understanding batterers' behavior and treatment, there is ample evidence that anger is involved in episodes of domestic violence.

Comorbidity Issues

To be sure, in relation to this series of anger-response criteria, assessing the extent of anger issue and the health needs of patients would depend on more than their status.

Conditions like thought disorder, personality disorder, depression, PTSD, learning disability, head injury or substance abuse disorder are often comorbid with anger problems. The treatment of cognitive behavioral anger is primarily an adjunctive treatment, not meant to be sufficient to address the broader clinical needs of a client. The "brevity" of this adjunctive treatment will then vary depending on the degree of impairment presented by other clinical conditions under which the problem of anger is nestled, as well as the frequency, intensity, duration and mode of expression of anger. In the aforementioned analysis, though, we have tried to demarcate the aspects of rage responses and offer insight on the nature of the anger problem; this has consequences for the psychological services required to resolve the pathology of anger. To the extent that anger dysregulation — often becoming angry, being angry at high intensity, remaining angry for prolonged periods, and either expressing anger in aggressive behavior or repeatedly suppressing it without acting to resolve conflict situations — constitutes the main problem of the client, CBT anger treatment can very well serve as the primary clinical service. Most often, however, people with persistent rage disorders have numerous health conditions, and are as resistant to seeking care as they are to any ways to invade their personal environment.

CHAPTER SEVEN

Mindfulness Based Cognitive Behavioral Therapy

According to the fourth edition of the Mental Disorders Diagnostic and Predictive Manual (DSM-IV - TR, American Psychiatric Association [APA], 2000), Major Depressive Disorder (MDD) is a depression condition marked by one or more major depressive symptoms (i.e., at least two weeks of unstable depression or lack of confidence or enjoyment in almost all activity), followed by at least four subsequent periods. MDD poses a major threat to mental health, with a lifetime prevalence measured at 17 percent (Kessler, Bergland, & Demler, 2005). Similarly, individuals suffering from one depressive episode will experience on average four major depressive episodes lasting for 20 weeks over their lifetime.

According to a recently released study of 245,000 in sixty nations by the World Health Organization, MDD is more harmful to everyday health than chronic diseases such as angina, arthritis, asthma and diabetes. It is projected that MDD causes the fourth-largest ill health burden among all diseases worldwide and will push into second place by 2020. Despite successful medication and psychotherapies, fewer than half of patients achieve remission, and recurrence in individuals who are not fully recovering is more likely. For these reasons, both basic and treatment research efforts are homing in on identifying vulnerability factors associated with the onset and maintenance of depression, as well as mechanisms promoting relapse risk.

Meditation and other mental training exercises derived from the 2,500-year Buddhist and Hindu traditions represent one potentially fruitful area of study with the potential to expand contemporary models of depression as well as complement existing treatments for medication and psychotherapy. Over the past 30 years there has been a growing trend in meditation , yoga, and other mental conditioning techniques originating from Hindu and Buddhist practice. With the emergence of affective neuroscience, a sub-discipline in the fields of psychology, psychiatry, and neurology that examines the neural bases of mood and emotion, the use of these practices has doubled in recent years. The union of these Eastern practices under the scrutiny of a Western scientific approach to investigation has led to the development of new and effective clinical interventions aimed at restoring psychological functioning and reducing human suffering across a wide range of diseases, while at the same time offering a fascinating glimpse of neural correlates of emotional processing and how factors (e.g. One activity that has been shown to have saliency in researching and treating MDD is meditation on mindfulness. Kabat-Zinn, a contemporary theorist, practitioner and teacher, describes awareness as a process of attracting a certain quality of attention to the moment-by-moment experience, "by paying particular attention. Intentionally, at this moment in time. Unjudgmentally. "It is believed that the ability to cultivate a state of mindfulness arises with the practice of Buddhist mental training exercises, such as meditation.

The purpose of this chapter is to offer a modern scientific account of MDD as a bio-psychosocial disorder enhanced by concepts of mindfulness and acceptance. By doing so, we establish linkages with the mainstream cognitive behavioral paradigm, which, also early on, interpreted MDD as arising from an inability to develop metacognitive abilities that facilitate balanced emotional transition. After reviewing evidence associating metacognitive awareness with depression, we postulate that this emphasis on metacognition has created fertile ground instead of cognitive content per se to incorporate principles of awareness into the etiology and treatment model. We conclude the chapter by reviewing findings from studies that include carefulness-enriched treatments for MDD and other emotional disorders, and then frame issues facing our field, given the promising beginning of incorporating principles of carefulness into our models.

The Traditional Cognitive Behavioral Model of the Psychopathology and Treatment of Major Depressive Disorder

Cognitive models of diathesis-stress depression have strengthened our knowledge of the disorder's etiology, diagnosis and care in a variety of ways. These theories posit that vulnerability to depression arises through experiences in early life that lead one to develop a depressogenic world view. Specifically, the Theory of Reformulated Learned Helplessness (Abramson et al . , 1978) and the Theory of Hopelessness (Abramson et al., 1989) both conceptualize vulnerability to depression in terms of a depressogenic or pessimistic explanatory style (specifically, the tendency to view negative events as arising from stable, global and internal reasons). Similarly, Beck 's depression theory argues that vulnerability to depression is associated with dysfunctional attitudes and negative self, world, and future schemes.

Traditional Targets of Cognitive Therapy of Depression

Cognitive behavioral depression theories have guided and inspired attempts to establish psychotherapies and include strategies for teaching individuals how to recognise and criticize depressive causal attributions for real events or negative thinking. Empirical findings consistently promote the effectiveness of the depression cognitive therapy. The basic processes of improvement in cognitive therapy remain a matter of significant concern in the field and the nature of the current chapter is beyond a comprehensive examination. Late in the cognitive therapy tradition, the focus of the debate was about which aspects of perception were the most suitable goals for cognitive therapy improvement. Hollon and his colleagues distinguish two main types of cognitions: cognitive structures and cognitive products. Cognitive constructs reflect "the way information is represented in memory" Cognitive structures play an active part in informational processing. Cognitive schemas (or schemas) are a type of cognitive structure that is important for depression cognitive theories and therapies. In contrast, cognitive products represent conscious thoughts that are directly accessible, such as self-statements, automatic thoughts and causal attributions. Such products are the result of using cognitive structures to process sensory input information.

With regard to cognitive stress treatment, the difference between cognitive constructs and cognitive goods is important. For example , researchers warn that targeting cognitive goods would possibly provide little therapeutic benefit, since symptomatic therapies lead to these interventions. This issue has propelled approaches to treatment which address cognitive structure. For example, Beck and colleagues (1979) explicitly state that changes in cognitive structures or core schemas in cognitive therapy represent critical mechanisms for change. Likewise, Safran et al . (1986) contend that cognitive change efforts should focus on core processes. In addition, Beck (1984) warned that depressed individuals would remain vulnerable to relapse when the cognitive underlying structures were not targeted and changed. More recently, Hollon et al . (2005) found that patients diagnosed with cognitive therapy, which were unrealistically hopeful or enthusiastic in their outlook, in turn had fewer enduring therapeutic results relative to patients who developed a more rational attitude. Thus, throughout the history of cognitive depression therapy, the discussion has at times focused on whether cognitive content changes were sufficient to produce the therapeutic benefits, or rather whether the true mechanism of action was a more structural change in the relationship with cognitive material. Clearly, the question of pathways for cognitive improvement has remained a subject of considerable concern and, more importantly, has provided resources to further elucidate the metacognitive essence of cognitive therapy.

Metacognitive Approaches to Emotional Processing

"Metacognition refers to one's knowledge of or anything related to one's own cognitive processes" Metacognition fundamentally reflects a neural mechanism that promotes sense-making and change of our lives. In many systems of psychotherapy, transforming meaning remains an important focus especially outside of traditional cognitive therapy. However, cognitive behavioral approaches have long debated and studied emotional processing, particularly in relation to fear and anxiety. A common thread tying these approaches together is an appreciation that the processing and integration of information, particularly emotionally laden information from multiple pathways, results in the making and transformation of meaning. In specific, researchers usually differentiate overt, higher-order mental processing that involves predominantly rule-based learning from slow, associational processing that involves classically conditioned learning. Such transmission pathways in his neurobiological model of emotions relate closely to the higher and lower routes suggested by LeDoux (1996). Similarly, Greenberg and Safran (1987) have stressed the importance of exploring various emotional channels within the therapy. Thus, these multilevel models of emotion processing, drawing from approaches to cognitive science, stress the qualitative aspects of information typically generated from higher and lower order emotional pathways and the way in which they are retrieved.

Metacognitive Model of Depression

Although recent years have seen an increasing emphasis on metacognitive factors in depression etiology and treatment (e.g., Teasdale, 1999), Beck's (1984) model of etiology and treatment was inherently metacognitive in nature. For example, Ingram and Hollon claimed that "cognitive therapy relies on helping individuals transition to a guided, strenuous form of processing that is metacognitive in nature and focuses on cognition relevant to depression" and that "the long-term efficacy of cognitive therapy may lie in training patients to undertake this process in the face of potential stress." According to the theory of Teasdale, susceptibility to depression is associated with the degree to which a person relies on a specific mind mode to avoid the other modes. Teasdale (1999) postulated that the risk of recurrence and recurrence to depression is related to the ease in which depressogenic, ruminative treatment is restored, rather than the presence or absence of specific negative beliefs or assumptions.

Metacognitive Processing and Depression

Cognitive subsystems interacting and vulnerability to depression

Multilevel mind theory by Barnard and Teasdale (1991), the Interacting Cognitive Sub-Systems (ICS), describes three mind modes open to individuals for the processing of information. The mindless style of emoting is characterized by solely emotional, sensory-driven responses without paying attention to "the bigger picture." The conceptualizing-doing style is synonymous with thinking that includes concentrating on intellectual information and interpretation, such as going shopping for groceries. Finally, the self-experiencing state of thinking refers to the awareness of emotions, perceptions and inner and outer experiences, resulting in a convergence of consciousness. The ICS theory seeks to account for the cognitive and emotional way in which human beings process the information.

According to the principle of ICS, mental wellbeing is correlated with the capacity to disengage from a single mind state or to flexibly switch between mind state. Accordingly, an optimal state is one in which individuals can deftly switch between the three identified mind modes based on environmental conditions. Still, each of these mind modes has special relevance to one's vulnerability to depression.

The mindful mode of experiencing/being within the ICS framework is characterized by cognitive-affective inner exploration, the use of present feelings as a guide to problem-solving and a non-evaluative awareness of present subjective-self-experience. In this mode, feelings, sensations, and thoughts are sensed directly as aspects of subjective experience, rather than as objects of conceptual thinking. Of the three different processing configurations, the single configuration conducive to emotional processing is the mindful experience/being mode. Emotional processing involves integrating new elements to create new alternative patterns of schematic meanings within the existing schema. The mode of mind that is mindful / experiencing is thought to be related to emotional wellbeing.

In contrast, the mindless emoting and conceptualizing/doing mind modes are theorized to confer vulnerability to depression according to the ICS theory. Individuals in a mindless mode of emoting have a conscious experience characterized as immersed in and identified with their affective reactions, with little self-awareness, inner exploration, or reflection. This mode may be contrasted with the awareness of the subjective experiences that characterize the mindful mode of experiencing/being. One form of mindless mode of emoting is cognitive reactivity, defined as a change in one or more cognitive indices in response to a challenge to emotional evocation. Psychological vulnerability has been associated with cognitive reactivity and increased risk of depression. Thus, Teasdale (1999) postulates that the risk of recurrence and relapse to depression is related to the ability of an individual to alternate in a flexible manner between processing modes, depending on environmental input. Thus, individuals who remain rigidly in a mindless mode of emoting or conceptualization / doing are subject to increased risk for negative states of affect. However, when individuals vacillate between conceptualizing/doing and mindless processing modes of emoting it is particularly problematic. Although not rigidly linked to one processing mode, a rapid switch between these modes leaves individuals vulnerable to what Teasdale (1999) refers to as a "depressive interlock," involving a feedback loop of ruminative self-reflection, depression, and its causes and consequences. Depressive interlocking occurs when the mind becomes dominated by using negative, depressive content to process information. This type of thinking creates a negative feedback loop hypothesized to maintain depression and re-establish it at the time of recurrence and relapse. Teasdale believes that this style of behavior is similar to the conceptualisation of suicidal rumination by Nolen-Hoeksema (1991). Therefore, any treatment for depression should result in more time spent in mindful-experiencing mode and the ability to switch more flexibly between mind modes depending on the context of emotional processing, when considering Teasdale's ICS model.

Metacognitive Awareness

A central component of depression's metacognitive model is the construction of metacognitive awareness, broadly defined as the ability to experience negative thoughts / feelings as mental events rather than being synonymous with one's self. This broadened perspective on negative events is encoded in memory and thus represents a more adaptive way to relate when they arise to negative thoughts. Individuals elevated in metacognitive sensitivity, comparison with individuals poor in metacognitive knowledge, are more likely to escape depression and its sequelae as they disidentify with suicidal thinking and emotions that occur in the midst of a challenging circumstance. Many measures of metacognitive cognition have gained recognition in correlational, prospective, retrospective, and clinical trials in recent years.

Teasdale and colleagues (2002) examined the relationship between reduced metacognitive awareness of vulnerability to depression, and the effects of cognitive therapy on metacognitive awareness of relapse of depression. The first study revealed that euthymic patients with a depression history demonstrated significantly lower levels of meta-cognitive awareness compared with non-depressed controls matched by age and gender. In the second study, Teasdale et al . (2002) found that in patients with severe depression, lower rates of metacognitive memory reaching five months prior to baseline measurement indicated faster relapse. This finding is consistent with the hypothesis that, within a broader perspective, the ability to relate to depressive thoughts and feelings reduces the likelihood of future recurrence. These researchers also found that in comparison with the comparison treatment, cognitive therapy increased accessibility to metacognitive sets with respect to negative thoughts and sensations. Differences between cognitive therapy and comparative therapy were shown only in memories encoded during the treatment phase and not in previous memories, suggesting that changes in metacognitive awareness as a result of cognitive therapy reflected the effects of cognitive therapy on the encoding of depressive experiences rather than the artifactual effects of cognitive therapy on the depressin pathway Consequently, cognitive therapy succeeds in increasing metacognitive awareness, and these metacognitive gains are associated with positive results.

Decentering

Another construct closely related to metacognitive awareness is decentering, which represents one's ability to observe thoughts and feelings as temporary, objective events in the mind as opposed to the necessarily true reflections of one's self. From a decentered viewpoint, The reality of the moment is not absolute, unchangeable or unchangeable ». For eg, a person engaging in decentering would say, "I think I'm feeling depressed right now" rather than "I'm depressed." Decentering is present-focused and includes taking a non-judgmental and supportive approach about thoughts and emotions. Although the concept of decentering can be found in traditional cognitive therapy, Teasdale and colleagues suggest that it has been viewed primarily as "a means to change the content of thought rather than as. The primary mechanism of therapeutic change. "In other words, both Beck and Teasdale agree that decentering has always been included in cognitive therapy as a concept and capacity that successfully cultivates depressed patients. However, a primary difference between cognitive depression therapy as delivered by Beck and colleagues (1979) and Teasdale and colleagues (2002) is that for Beck, decentering is an ability that allows an individual to make a significant change in one's core beliefs, while for Teasdale, decentering is in and of itself the ability that produces a lasting relief from depression.

Explanatory Style and Flexibility

Explanatory flexibility in determining causal causes for adverse outcomes is a metacognitive expansion to explanatory type, the perceptual diathesis at the root of the principle of depression's reformulated taught helplessness. Explanatory flexibility, broadly constructed, is the ability to view events with a balance of historical and contextual information. Unlike the explanatory type, the Attributional Type Questionnaire assesses explanatory versatility, a self-report metric in which respondents are confronted with simulated adverse incidents and are asked to document the key cause of the case, as well as numerical scores on the causal aspects of internality, consistency, and globality. Whereas explanatory style is scored as the sum or average of the attributional dimensions, with higher scores indicating a more depressogenic style, explanatory flexibility is calculated as the intra-individual standard deviation for negative events on the ASQ dimensions of stability and globality. A small standard deviation is considered to be a rigid response, interpreting a large standard deviation as a flexible response.

To date, studies have shown a relationship between explanatory flexibility and depression in a number of contexts. Fresco and colleagues have shown that explanatory style and explanatory flexibility are relatively uncorrelated and that lower explanatory flexibility scores are not merely proxies for extreme explanatory style responses (Moore & Fresco, 2007), that explanatory flexibility is associated with simultaneous symptoms of depression and anxiety (Fresco, Williams & Nugent, 2). Moreover, a series of studies have shown that an emotional provocation can generate reactivity in explanatory flexibility for individuals considered at risk of reactivity, and that this reactivity interacts with interfering negative life events to predict symptoms of depression eight weeks and six months later (Moore & Fresco, 2009). In addition, the reactivity of explanatory flexibility in the direction of reduced flexibility was associated with reduced parasympathetic tone during the mood priming challenge and lower parasympathetic tone recovery following the mood priming challenge.

In the form of acute therapy for major depressive disorder, two studies have explored the link of causal versatility to depression. Specifically, in a secondary review of the cognitive disorder therapy dismantling research performed by Jacobson and colleagues (1996), results indicated that suicidal individuals reacting to behavioral stimulation demonstrated greater explanatory versatility benefits, whereas depressed patients obtaining a combination of behavioral activation + a disagreement regarding negative automatic though in addition, the combination of improved explanatory stability and decreased explanatory negative style projected better security from recurrence during the two year follow-up period. Therefore, the behavioural stimulation component of the therapy may have induced improvements in the cognitive framework (i.e., flexibility), while the conflict over suicidal thinking may have affected changes in cognitive material, all of which indicated improved safety from relapse.

Fresco, Ciesla, Marcotte, and Jarrett (2009a) performed secondary study in another recent randomized clinical trial exploring the benefits in cognitive stress treatment. In the initial study, Jarrett and colleagues (2001) treated MDD patients with cognitive therapy (CT) for 20 sessions in an open-label fashion. Respondents were then automatically allocated to 10 additional CT sessions administered over an eight-month period (Continuation Phase CT) or a diagnosis purely for evaluation. Patients were then followed up for a further 16 months with no further research medication. Findings showed that patients receiving CT continuity exhibited lower rates of recurrence and relapse relative to patients receiving no additional CT. In Fresco and colleagues' secondary analysis (2009a), findings indicated that gains in explanatory flexibility during the acute, open-label CT phase preceded and predicted drops in self-report and clinician-assessed symptoms of depression. Continuation phase CT, however, was not associated with further gains in explanatory flexibility. Similarly, the study's follow-up period did not correlate predictive versatility with the rates of recurrence and relapse. Consequently, gains in explanatory flexibility provided by behavioral approaches can result in reduced relapse and recurrence and hence more lasting effects on treatment.

Extreme Responding

Another metacognitive aspect correlated with signs of depression is rigidity in assigning causal causes to the ASQ for inference to negative or positive events. Specifically, several studies have found that extreme responses to the ASQ are associated with poor clinical outcomes for depressed patients. In one study by Teasdale and colleagues (2001), 158 patients with residual depression currently being treated with antidepressant drugs were randomly assigned either alone or with cognitive therapy (CT) to receive continuation of the drug with clinical management. Participants were asked to report on the ASQ attributions before and after the treatment. Extreme response (i.e., either "totally disagree" or "totally agree"), but not the response content (i.e. reaction to specific items) predicted a relapse. Beevers and colleagues (2003) found similar results in that poor change in extreme response predicted a shorter amount of time until depressive symptoms returned for asymptomatic or partially remitted depression in individuals treated. Evidence was also received from Petersen and colleagues (2007) for the association between extreme response and depression, who observed that drug-only therapy for severely depressive patients was associated with an improved incidence of extreme response to the ASQ due to no meaningful improvement in reaction when treated with CBT. In addition, extreme response to the ASQ predicted a significantly higher probability of depressive remission in these patients. Therefore, cognitive therapy tends to have an effect on it by reducing the probability of severe reaction which in turn results in fewer depressive symptoms.

Metacognition Summary

Numerous work carried out by many different scholars agree on the role that metacognitive factors play in treating major depressive disorder. There are two findings which are particularly relevant at this point. First, the ability to approach emotionally evocative situations with metacognitive awareness seems important to prevent relapse. Second, this metacognitive awareness is reflected in several constructs that have shown a relationship to depression: decentering, explanatory flexibility and extreme response. Specifically, existing psychosocial treatments can be enhanced by targeting those capabilities to achieve acute and lasting gains in treatment. Many questions about metacognition and wellbeing remain unanswered. A significant topic being hotly discussed, though, is that metacognitive knowledge can be developed more readily than for traditional psychosocial therapies. Part of the answer to this question stems from the observation that these metacognitive abilities bear a close resemblance to the abilities which are believed to arise from the practice of mental training exercises derived from Buddhist and Hindu traditions. The conceptual similarities have led clinical scientists (e.g., Segal, Williams, & Teasdale, 2002) and affective neuroscientists (e.g., Lutz, Slagter, Dunne, & Davidson, 2008) to notice such exercises in mental education. Concentration practices, such as meditation on consciousness, involve focusing attention on a particular mental or sensory activity, such as repeated imagery, sensations, sounds, or mantras. It is assumed that cultivating such a practice fosters metacognitive awareness. We are now moving to a study of attempts to infuse behavioral Buddhist conditioning techniques into western MDD therapies.

Using Mindfulness Meditation to Promote Metacognitive Awareness

Multilevel theory of mind by Barnard and Teasdale (1991) suggests that the attentive method of experiencing/being is the most likely form of thought to contribute to permanent mental improvements, which in turn has consequences for the avoidance of relapse of depression. In addition, cognitive therapy may foster a mindful mode of experiencing/being. One facet of cognitive therapy primarily entails encouraging people to build and store alternate schematic models in memory that can be activated by the same patterns of knowledge that usually cause depressogenic schematic models. A second dimension allows individuals learn to disengage skills from differences between conceptualizing/doing mode and excessive emotion mode (i.e. suicidal interlock) to work in conscious experience/being / space.

Although cognitive therapy may contribute to the development of these capacities, Teasdale (1999) indicates that individuals will actually benefit from developing "mind control" techniques to escape suicidal interlocking during times of possible relapse. Interventions composed of carefulness exercises (e.g., transcendental meditation, Maharishi [1963]; mindfulness-based stress reduction, Kabat-Zinn [1990]; and mindfulness-based cognitive therapy, Segal, Williams & Teasdale [2002]) have emerged in recent years as viable supplements to standard Western medical and psychological practices. Mindfulness was described as a moment-by-moment, non-judgmental awareness of the experience. Mindfulness is an active process by which attention to the present moment is cultivated in a way that allows for a complete and meaningful experience of all aspects of that moment, without avoiding, judging, or ruminating on certain features. Participants are advised to use mindfulness-based stress management methods to incorporate relaxation into their lives by reflecting on simple activities such as breathing, body movements, and the movement of emotions in one's mind. Kabat-Zinn defines the following as the pillars of mindfulness: non-judgment of the moment and of yourself, flexibility, the mind of the novice (i.e., openness to viewing it as a new experience), trust in yourself and one's emotions, non-striving (not having a reason to achieve something), appreciation of the moment and yourself, and letting go (or non-attachment). Such behaviors, when contemplating the metacognitive paradigm of Teasdale (1999), help to diminish a disconnected, goal-oriented emphasis (conceptualizing/doing mind mode) and a state of mind in which feelings are all-encompassing and felt without awareness (mindless emotion). MBSR uses strategies such as deep meditation, body scans and careful walking to develop a mindful-experiencing mentality, incorporating all facets of perception into a cohesive whole. Originally designed to lessen some of the mental and physical sufferings associated with chronic pain.

Mindfulness-based cognitive therapy (MBCT) borrows MBSR-derived techniques while cognitive-behavioral interventions are taught in conjunction to specifically target vulnerability to depressive relapse. MBCT is an eight-week group program run with up to 12 patients recovering from recurring depression. The program 's aim is for patients to develop awareness of negative thinking patterns such as avoiding unwanted thoughts , feelings, and body sensations, and to respond more effectively to them (Ma & Teasdale 2004). The purpose of the mindfulness skills is to help participants accept these negative patterns of thinking and to respond to these patterns in intentionally and skillfully. In this way, MBCT cultivates a decentered relation to negative thoughts and feelings in the service of moving from a "automatic pilot" mode to an emotional processing mode of "being." The counseling starts by recognizing the destructive unconscious thought typical of those undergoing recurrent periods of depression, and by incorporating certain simple methods of mindfulness. In the second session , participants are encouraged to understand more generally the reactions they have to experiences in life, and more specifically the experiences of mindfulness. In the third session, mindful awareness is fostered by teaching respiratory techniques to focus attention on the present moment. Experiencing the moment in the fourth session without being hooked, aversive, or distracted is viewed as a means of avoiding relapse. Session five is used to promote acceptance of one's experience without holding on to it, and session six is used to describe thoughts as "just thoughts." In the final sessions, participants are taught how to take care of themselves, prepare for relapse and expand their practices of mindfulness into daily life. In a recent study examining the relationships between training in mindfulness, meta-cognitive awareness and depressive symptoms, Carmody, Baer, and colleagues (2009) found that training in mindfulness led to increased awareness and decenteration. Further to the point, both variables expected a substantial decrease in psychiatric problems, indicating to the writers that concentration and decentering are closely related.

CHAPTER EIGHT

CBT for Anxiety Disorder

BT, especially in vivo exposure, obtains the most reliable outcomes for the treatment of severe phobias, but it is correlated with high dropout levels and poor approval of therapy. So it may be desirable to combine the cognitive and behavioral components. Cognitive restructuring is effective in the treatment of claustrophobia alone and in combination with in vivo exposure, and cognitive restructuring alone is effective in the treatment of dental and flying phobias. CBT has more positive effects for treating common phobias than hypnotherapy and medicine. For certain phobias, CBT has demonstrated long-term retention of increases from 12.0 to 13.8 months. CBT demonstrates mild to strong total efficacy for overcoming social phobia. The most common combination of CBT components is cognitive rehabilitation plus stimulation, but inconsistent results make the dominance of this combination over other combinations, or solo elements, uncertain. One analysis showed CBT by itself and CBT plus pharmacotherapy were similarly successful. Complicating the data is the fact that each study defines CBT and exposure differently. However, community CBT is the most cost-effective and tolerable therapy, and the medication of choice for social phobia should also be considered. CBT's long-term success for social phobia has been proven for up to 12 months.

The total efficacy of CBT is overwhelming and well-supported for OCD. Cognitive therapy and ERP are two aspects of well-defined CBT strategies which are frequently merged. No support is given for the incremental benefit of adding cognitive techniques to BT; typically, BT outperforms CBT. However, cognitive approaches improve therapy tolerability, inspire clients and help them control the elements dependent on sensitivity. Aside from BT, CBT has not been compared to other psychotherapies. There has not been a clear contrast of pharmacotherapy and CBT and definitive conclusions can not be made. A limited volume of evidence suggests that any medication alone may be preferable to a mixture of pharmacotherapy and CBT. Insufficient data are available to report on the continued efficacy of CBT, and to distinguish between PD and PDA performance.

CBT 's controlled and unchecked absolute efficacy for PD / PDA has been amply demonstrated. Exposure and cognitive restructuring are the typical constituents of CBT for PD / PDA. Adding cognitive components to behavioral components for PD / PDA treatment does not result in incremental value in terms of reduced anxiety, but in terms of reduced symptoms of depression and attrition rates. CT is superior to RT but no other comparisons have been reviewed between psychotherapies and CBT. There is a mix of evidence for the relative effectiveness of pharmacotherapy and CBT; some studies have considered the two to be similarly effective; some have reported divergent outcomes based on the outcome factors examined; and others have found proof of CBT dominance over pharmacotherapy. There are also mixed results with respect to the relative efficacy of CBT alone and a combined intervention in CBT – pharmacotherapy. Lastly, CBT has the best cost profile of the interventions, and the long-term effectiveness of CBT has been demonstrated up to 16.8 months on average.

Chronic PTSD has received the most research attention, but the literature on CBT treatment efficacy has also examined immediate post-trauma experiences and acute PTSD. TFCBT (that is, exposure and trauma-focused cognitive techniques) is the most widely studied form of CBT. TFCBT and EMDR both have demonstrated controlled absolute efficacy for chronic PTSD, are superior to "other therapies," and are not significantly different from one another. TFCBT can only be considered tentatively superior to pharmacotherapy (i.e., paroxetine) for the treatment of chronic PTSD, due to limited and inconclusive evidence. CBT 's controlled absolute efficacy for GAD treatment is well-established for the short term; however, due to insufficient data, long-term results are indeterminate. Compared with CBT, the relative efficacy of pharmacotherapy is not clear; the data is inconsistent, based on the particular effects measured. For at least one study, however, scholars surmised that CBT is better tolerated than pharmacotherapy. CBT has shown dominance over post-treatment and 6-month follow-up psychodynamic intervention, modest dominance over positive intervention, inconsistent outcomes relative to BT, and comparable effectiveness compared to RT. In the meta-analyses we reviewed, the relative effectiveness of CBT compared to combined CBT and pharmacotherapy was not stated. CBT for GAD recovery literature covers several aspects under the CBT rubric, including instruction in anxiety reduction, cognitive rehabilitation, acute awareness, self-controlled desensitization, RT/reading, CT alone, and BT alone.

At this point, cognitive behavioral therapy (CBT) could be the leading choice for treating many forms of anxiety. This has been found to be as effective in treating panic disorder and phobias as prescription drugs, and it also shows considerable potential for treating obsessive-compulsive disorder and post-traumatic stress disorder. It's not a "wonder drug," or magic cure, however. Cognitive behavioural therapy for the diagnosis of anxiety illness is a relatively complicated procedure that often involves ongoing and patient constructive involvement, as well as instruction in most cases by a professional teacher or therapist.

For starters, cognitive behavioral therapy is not one thing, but rather a general term for a number of similar but distinct therapies, such as Rational Emotional Behavior Therapy, Rational Behavior Therapy, Rational Living Therapy, Cognitive Therapy, and Dialectic Behavior Therapy.

However, one thing all these therapies share is the belief that what actually controls our feelings and behaviors is our thoughts — not external things like people, situations, and events. And if we can change the way we think, even if the external factors do not change, we can feel better and react differently. The role of the therapist is to teach the clients how to recognize and challenge and consciously correct their own irrational and self-destructive beliefs.

CBT is an educational process that holds that they can be unlearned to the extent that emotional and behavioral reactions are learned. The purpose of counseling is to help clients unlearn unhealthy responses and replace them with new ways of responding to sources of stress and anxiety. CBT therapists are focused on teaching rational self-control skills. Counseling sessions rely on conversation and structured interviews to help patients identify the specific thoughts and situations that disturb them, rationally analyze those factors, and learn specific techniques and concepts to defuse them when they grow. Homework and reading tasks are an integral part of the process and are crucial to making CBT a therapy that is fairly short-term and time-limited. Homework and techniques commonly used in CBT include keeping a diary of events and the feelings, thoughts and behaviors that they trigger; asking questions and challenging the faulty or unrealistic perceptions and beliefs of the patient; learning to overcome avoidance and confront challenging situations and activities; training in techniques of relaxation, mindfulness and distraction.

Exposure therapy and desensitization for anxiety disorders are essential features of most CBTs. Once the client and therapist have identified the triggers of anxiety and their associated feelings and thoughts, they work to break the pattern of response by recreating or evoking those events and feelings under controlled conditions. Starting by teaching calming methods, meditation, or breathing exercises that will help the patient to manage their apprehension and anxiety during the exposure phase is important. Gradual repetitive conditions cause the patient to cope with reduced stress thresholds and gradually build up until he or she is no longer responsive to the previous stimuli.

CBT is a technique that is deeply empowering and is one reason why it is so effective in treating anxiety-related disorders. Understanding the relationship between your mental and physical symptoms and knowing that you have tools and techniques to manage these symptoms can significantly reduce anticipatory anxiety-which is often the key difference between occasional disturbing but essentially normal episodes of anxiety or even panic, and a full-blown chronic anxiety disorder that weakens.

How Can CBT Eliminate Your anxiety Attacks?

Many of us agree that the circumstances we encounter and our everyday encounters are the causes of fear, panic, and depression. For example, if you drive your car, and you get an anxiety attack when you get on a highway, you probably think your anxiety is caused by driving up the highway. In not true, this. According to CBT the intensity of your emotions is determined by your thoughts and set of beliefs.

Cognitive behavioural therapy gives you easy strategies to avoid dead episodes of fear and anxiety in their path.

CBT is the only method that can permanently cure anxiety and panic disorder, because it uses scientifically verified strategies to relieve long-term anxiety. Other popular treatments — such as medication, herbal remedies, breathing exercises, and more — usually only treat symptoms of anxiety and don't treat the root of the problem — your brain and your thinking!

Cognitive Behavioral Therapy for Treatment of Anxiety Disorder

Cognitive-behavioral therapy, or CBT, works on the minds and behaviors of the patient to change how they feel and how they react to "negative" situations.

CBT is based on the assumption that the way we react to things is conditioned, and that the conditioned responses can be changed by unlearning them.

CBT aims to identify the patterns of thinking that negatively affect the life of the patient, and to find more resourceful ways of thinking or self-talking. Examples of distorted mindsets include:

• Should / must think: turn your interests and desires into pure necessities. Some examples of this kind of thinking include: "I have to get this," "this shouldn't have happened," "this person should have been nice to me."

• Overgeneralization: you see a single unwanted event as a permanent pattern of malaise. For instance: somebody doesn't treat you well and you think "I can never please people," even though the other person has treated you badly because he or she wasn't in good mood.

• Magnification and minimisation: the negatives are exaggerated and the positive discounted. You 're driving and turning in the wrong direction for starters. Then you think: "I have a terrible sense of direction" or "I'm such a bad driver," even if you rarely make this kind of "mistake."

• Mind-reading: You assume what others think of you without having any real evidence of your assumption.

We can see that such thought forms cause anxiety. Within you, you may find these patterns of thought to be factual, accurate or essential. Yet you don't have to look at them like this. We also see other people around us who act appropriately and do well in the circumstances outlined in the scenarios mentioned above, even when these situations happen far more times to these individuals than we would find reasonable individually. The way we respond is more about our programmed responses and values than anything else. CBT therapy is reciprocal, as the patient has to apply the strategies suggested by the psychiatrist in their everyday lives. The patient's activities may include writing down a list of the feelings, emotions and habits that happened in the patient's everyday life following traumatic events. The therapist will evaluate this list to determine distorted thoughts and more resourceful ways to tackle the particular issue. The therapy may also involve (gradual) imaginary exposure to a situation of fear or phobia, or exposure to real life.

The cause of the problem is not relevant for CBT, because it focuses on the "here and how," i.e., the thoughts and behaviors that cause the problem or contribute to it.

Although, other types of psychotherapy may take years for the benefits to come, CBT treatment usually lasts a couple of months.

Cure Your Anxiety Condition with CBT

The wide range of anxiety conditions, including panic disorder, obsessive compulsive disorder, post-traumatic stress disorder, generalized anxiety disorder, social anxiety disorder, and phobias, are permanently cured. Anxiety disorders plague 40 million American adults, ages 18 and older, according to the National Institute for Mental Health (NIMH). As we mull over the meaning of this staggering number, let 's look at the recommended treatment method, one that provides recovery for hundreds of thousands of patients.

Cognitive behavioural therapy is in essence a fusion of two separate approaches, all of which trace their origins back to the 1950s and 1960s — and their adoption by the psychiatric community during the 1970s and 1980s.

The American psychiatrist Aaron T. Beck developed cognitive therapy during the 1960's. Beck initially applied his approach to depression issues, then broadened his practice to include anxiety disorders. How it is that people interpret and assign meaning to their everyday lives is a process called cognition. Beck, disillusioned with conventional psychotherapeutic delving into the subconscious, believed that perception was the secret to successful treatment and would lead to meaningful healing, as his patients understood it.

Beck first found, while designing his treatment, that suicidal individuals embrace a pessimistic view of the environment during formative years — based on the death of a loved one, social disappointment, criticism by sources of power, depressive behaviors present in other important ones, plus a host of spontaneous adverse incidents. Very commonly, a distorted, subjective view of the world reinforces and nurtures this negative perception — for example, all-or-nothing thought, overgeneralization, and narrow beliefs that ignore important, concrete facts. Cognitive therapy postulates that distortions grow to disorders in a person's perspectives. It is a cognitive therapist's job to point these distortions out and to encourage change in the attitude of a sufferer.

Beginning in 1953, in the United States, behaviour modification made its debut in a groundbreaking effort led by B.F. Skinner. Skinner. In South Africa, the credit for pioneering work goes to Joseph Wolpe and his research group. Hans Eysenck has contributed to the development of such therapy in the United Kingdom.

Behavioral therapy is mainly based on functional analysis. Behavioral therapies have been used widely as a treatment for disorders of marriage, physical pain, fatigue, anorexia, psychological illness, drug misuse, psychiatric depression and anxiety.

Behavioral therapy focuses on the environment and its context and is data-driven and contextual. Behavioral therapy generally concerns the effect or outcome of behavior, behavior is regarded as objectively predictable; a person is handled as an individual without the complications of a mind-to-body approach, but partnerships, bidirectional experiences, are well taken into consideration.

The anxiety conditions were originally considered to be by-products of chemical imbalances and/or genetic predispositions. With those notions abandoned, learned behaviors were credited as the source of most conditions of anxiety. There was hope for a permanent cure, and cognitive therapy and behavioral therapy merged into cognitive behavioral therapy (CBT) in the 1990s. The common ground for these two therapies is to emphasize the "here and now" by focusing on symptom alleviation and replacing harmful, self-destructive behavior with beneficial beliefs and attitudes.

In the UK , the National Centre for Health and Professional Excellence proposes CBT as the best therapy for mental health issues such as OCD, post-traumatic stress disorder, bulimia, severe depression, and even chronic fatigue syndrome for the neurological condition. In the United States, CBT has gained recognition within the medical community, given our fascination with prescription solutions. Skilled, outcome-driven help is available to those who are seeking it.

CHAPTER NINE

CBT and Psychotherapy Integration

One of conflict and change, is the history of psychotherapy. The evolution of theory and practice has been both the product and the precipitator of rivalry and disagreement between those who instigate change and those who support the day's accepted theory. Early theories evolved largely through disagreements among the "talking cure" practitioners. Freud's disciples broke with him due to disagreements concerning both the nature of psychopathology and treatment techniques. Such disjunctive progress, in any new field, is understandable. Since research studies are scarce and the main means of exploration (as in early psychotherapy) are by unregulated experiments (e.g., patient case analysis), improvements in the field are eventually influenced by political discord and perception discrepancies.

Particularly in the early history of psychotherapy, the disputes that existed between theorists and practitioners were based inextricably on the fundamental issue of what constitutes proof of reality. Theoretical positions on psychotherapy have become sacrosanct, and scientific findings have been rejected because they have not fit the canons of one theoretical position or another. That situation created Babel 's virtual tower, and theories developed during the 1970s with unchecked abandonment. When the proliferation of different theoretical viewpoints reached its zenith in the 1980s, it would have been difficult to find any position on the nature or effectiveness of psychotherapy that would gain consensus, let alone the majority.

While the remnants of this discord remain, scientific findings are more acceptable than previously, and "evidence-based practice" has become the norm in medicine and other health care professions. Scientific inquiry and evidence derived through the scientific method gained ground as agents of change for the field. The disputes that emerge among practitioners, and between academic and practitioner cultures, discuss the importance of empirical evidence as knowledge baseless frequently than what constitutes "good" research. Most psychotherapists accept the value of scientific enquiry, at least in principle, even though they differ widely in what they consider acceptable scientific methods. However, despite this development, the acceptance of scientific findings as the basis for setting new directions or for deciding what is factual among practitioner therapists has been decidedly lagging. Indeed for many practitioners, the true test of a given psychotherapy rests on the observations of clinicians in both its theoretical logic and evidence, rather than data from sound scientific methods, even when the latter are available.

What practitioners accept as valid depends on both the methods and the strength of their opinions used to derive results. Practitioners prefer naturalistic research to randomized clinical studies, N = 1 or single-case studies to group designs, and individualization to group outcome measures. They also prefer to accept research that promotes the model they use over research that advocates alternate approaches to psychotherapy, or equivalence between methods. Since most research into psychotherapy fails to meet these values, psychotherapists are often quick to reject scientific findings that disagree with their own theoretical systems. So while the reasons given for rejecting scientific evidence may today be more sophisticated than in the past, it may not be less likely to happen.

The Emergence of Eclectic and Integrationist Views

Theorists who distance themselves from a mentor 's beliefs have also been viewed as pariahs. Consequently, it was not unusual to find that a practitioner of a particular theoretical orientation was quite ignorant of other theoretical schools' principles and practices. While this theoretical isolation may have motivated therapists and clinicians to refine and enhance the skills and techniques embraced by their respective theoretical orientations, its horizons and perspectives are also severely limited.

The psychotherapy field has evolved since the 1980s, in reaction to the rise of integrationist and multicultural views. This change was partially stimulated by the diversity of field opinion and the status of scientific evidence.

With over 400 different theories about the landscape of psychotherapy, the inescapable conclusion was that there was no single truth about psychopathology or psychotherapy. Practitioners were wary of theory and a profound disaffection for specific theoretical orientations grew. Dissatisfaction was compounded by the failure of scientific studies to firmly indicate any psychotherapy 's clear superiority relative to the others. Indeed, research showed that none of the psychotherapies adequately produced the systematic approaches that would contribute to the effective treatment of patients dealing with difficult and severe problems. Over the last few years, physicians have adopted ideas, strategies, and approaches from different fields of thought in an attempt to improve their own overall therapeutic efficacy.

Although the eclectic and integrationist movement caught on in the 1980s, its nucleus was in Thorne (1962), and Goldstein and Stein (1976) early works. Thorne's "eclectic" psychotherapy arose in counseling theory from a relational perspective. He argued that training doomed therapists to a single-method perspective that was inadequate to the variety of conditions, personalities, and needs of different patients, in much the same way that a carpenter who only had a screwdriver would be inadequately equipped to build a home. Thorne gave a diverse philosophical case with little basic institutional instructions. Goldstein and Stein, on the other hand, suggested that the selected procedures should be based on scientific evidence of effectiveness, and they presented examples of evidence-based treatments. Because of their scientific bent, these latter recommendations were largely derived from the literature on behavioral therapy, since at that point in time, behaviorism was the dominant approach in research. Modern eclecticism has become wider in scope but retained some of the values inherent in Thorne 's acceptance of procedures from a variety of perspectives, and in Goldstein and Stein's admonition to let scientific evidence dictate the methods of application rather than theory.

Surveys indicate that most North American mental health professionals identify with some form of eclecticism, or what is more commonly referred to as "integration," since the term implies a systematic application of concepts and techniques spawned by a variety of psychotherapies and pathology theories. As documented by membership of the Society for the Exploration of Psychotherapy Integration (SEPI), growth in the integrationist movement is international in scale.

Within the integrationist movement, at least four perspectives can be identified (Goldfried, 1995; Norcross & Goldfried, 1992; Norcross, Martin, Omer, & Pinsoff, 1996):

(1) Common Eclectic Factors,

(2) Theoretical inclusionism,

(3) and technological eclecticism;

(4) The eclecticism of a strategy.

Besides the unsystematic form of "haphazard eclecticism" to which many practitioners adhere, these approaches do exist. Haphazard eclecticism is based on some of the common convictions and statistical "evidence" that define the diverse tradition's more formal trends, most prominently the objective finding that different methods tend to be better tailored to different individuals. Unsystematic eclecticism, however, does not define the principles governing the merging of points of view, or a replicable procedure for selecting and applying treatments. This approach to eclecticism is widespread, but its effectiveness is hard to assess, as it varies between therapists as well as within them. Its effectiveness is inextricably bound up with the judgment and abilities of the therapist in question who applies it.

"Common factors eclecticism" relies among the more formal approaches on factors which are popular or close across approaches. The common psychotherapy approach to factors is different from the way one usually thinks about eclecticism. Common eclecticism factors accept that all effective psychotherapies are based on a core of basic ingredients, beyond which their distinctive effects are inconsistent or unpredictable. This approach seeks to recognize strategies or behaviors that occur in all effective therapies, and suggests that studies should examine the approaches and psycho-therapeutic relationships that facilitate or involve certain specific causes or attributes. This posture suggests that these common interventions will comprise effective psychotherapy. The therapist working within the growing approach to causes is never associated with particular approaches or methods, except those resulting in a congenial and loving partnership. Common therapist factors, such as most relationship-oriented therapists, create an accepting and non-threatening atmosphere in which the patient can explore problems. But unlike relationship-oriented therapies driven by specific psychopathology theories and changes, a certain type of therapy relationship is considered necessary and sufficient, and no more specific techniques or procedures are considered useful.

Though common factors are important elements of change, the contribution of specific classes of treatment interventions is supported by a growing research body. For example, recent research with manualized alcoholism treatments for cognitive — behavioral and family systems delivered in a couple format has suggested that both common treatment elements and specific interventions contribute to change. More specifically, components of the treatment appear to operate in a complex manner, independently and/or in interaction. In addition, the balance of common to specific elements of treatment exerts positive or attenuating effects depending on the treatment phase, the type of treatment given and the time of follow-up after treatment.

The preponderance of systematic eclectic hypotheses tackles the nature and variation of patients and therapies (aptitude x clinical experiences, or ATIs) by structuring and systematizing prescribed therapeutic interventions, since optimizing access to this particular mix of therapeutic variables better reduces the difficulties of patients (Stricker & Gold, 1996). These initiatives are driven at one end by what is termed "abstract integrationism" and at the other end by "scientific eclecticism." Among these poles are the conceptual eclectics, which combine all abstract ideas and methods at the level of behavioral effect action approaches and values. All three approaches are more systematic than either haphazard eclecticism, or common eclecticism factors. They share a common goal of guiding the therapist through decisions on which procedures to apply, who, and when. They identify the range of procedures to be used, and the patient or temporal and situational indications that index their maximum impact point. The theoretical integration movement, at the broadest level, attempts to amalgamate at least two theoretical viewpoints but leaves the specific techniques and procedures to the judgment of the clinician. These approaches see good theory as the avenue for developing good techniques; they contrast those approaches, which are often referred to in nature as either "eclectic" or "strategic."

The term "integration" has a set of meanings that go beyond the psychotherapy theories of interdigitation. For example, when you refer to an integrated personality in which the component traits, needs, wants, perceptions, values, emotions, and impulses are in a stable state of harmony and communication, it can refer to the quality of one's personality. An integrated person is one who is entire in terms of overall functioning and well-being. Integration in psychotherapy requires harmonious attempts to link affective, emotional, therapeutic, and program approaches to psychotherapy under a common framework, and to apply this philosophy to the treatment of people, groups, and families. This notion goes beyond any single theory or set of techniques and incorporates various models of human working.

Theoretical integration requires, at least superficially, the translation of concepts and methods from one psychotherapeutic system into the language and procedures of another. What always comes up is a new idea that incorporates elements of each of the previous ones. This theory encompasses identifying and standardizing effective concepts, terms and methods, and includes applying the resulting theoretical concepts to the research and application grist mill. Theoretical linkages among psychodynamic, behavioral, and cognitive approaches were made using an integration system.

Theoretical integration is the most abstract theoretical of the various systemic approaches. Theoretical integration attempts to bring together different theories through the development of a theoretical framework that can explain an individual's environmental, motivational, cognitive and affective domains that influence or are influenced by efforts to change; that is, theoretical integrative approaches combine two or more traditional theoretical orientations to produce a new person model Ideally these new forms of therapy capitalize on the strengths of each of the therapeutic elements.

Technical and strategic eclecticism is often seen as more clinically oriented and practical than theoretical integration. Strategic and technical approaches to eclectic therapy are less abstract than theoretical models of integration, and rely more on the utilization of specific techniques , procedures or principles. They define a variety of strategies (strategic eclecticism) or develop menus of psychotherapeutic interventions (technical eclecticism), irrespective of the theory which gave rise to these procedures. These types of integration are accomplished through a neutral perspective on the theories of change, or the adoption of a super-ordinate theory to replace or supersede the originals.

Technical and political eclectics are mainly concerned with the therapeutic efficacy of therapy methods, and do not pay any attention to the nature of the psychopathology and temperament hypotheses that give rise to these methods. These eclectics employ interventions from two or more psychotherapeutic systems and apply them to patients who have indicated qualities systematically and successively, using guidelines or heuristics based either on demonstrated or presumed clinical efficacy. This does not mean that the approaches in the technical eclectic tradition are devoid of theory; however, to the extent that theories are used, they are theories that link numerous empirical observations and rarely require the level of abstractness inherent in most traditional therapeutic change theories.

Multimodal therapy is the first and best known of the technically eclectic approaches (MMT; Lazarus, 1996). Around the same time, or in a structured series, MMT therapists apply various psychological methods and models based on the relative significance of the patient's symptoms. In other forms of technical eclecticism, prescriptive matching is dedicated to integrating a host of specific procedures, chosen from a wide range of menus, into a coherent and seamless treatment.

In the specificity of recommended procedures and techniques, the major distinction between technical eclecticism and strategic eclecticism is. Technical eclecticism provides a set of procedures that would suit a single individual or issue. Strategic eclecticism, by contrast, defines values and objectives but leaves the collection of approaches to the particular therapist's proclivities. The tacit or operating principle of technological eclecticism is that all techniques have a limited spectrum of applicability and application, whereas strategic eclecticism believes that all techniques can be employed in different forms and for different purposes, based on whether and by whom they are used.

Strategic therapy offers a middle ground between the technical emphasis of technological eclecticism and the theoretical integrationism abstract. Those approaches articulate therapeutic change principles that lead to general intervention strategies. The strategies are designed to implement the guiding principles, but the aim is to remain true to the principles rather than just focus on the specific techniques. As such, these approaches preserve individual therapist's flexibility in selecting particular techniques. They also maximize the use of techniques that are familiar and skilled to the therapist, without forgetting to use patient factors as reliable indicators for the selective application of various interventions. Typically such approaches provide clear interpretation of guiding principles that promote values of relationships, and elicit symptomatic and systemic changes. And they are perhaps the most versatile and realistic of the various approaches to integration: not as nuanced and comprehensive as integrationist approaches, and not as simple as technological eclecticism.

Though prescriptive psychotherapy sometimes resembles technical eclecticism, by constructing principles of change, it goes beyond the latter. The aim is a coherent treatment based on an overall view of the patient's presentation. Treatments based on explicit principles of change, such as those based on elaborate psychopathology theories, are most usefully integrated if researchable, do not rely on abstract concepts for which there is no measurement, and place few theory-driven bans on the use of various therapeutic techniques.

While most systematic eclectic psychotherapies span multiple theories, others use principles to guide the utilization of specific theories. Cognitive therapy (CT), for example, is appropriate for the application of diverse concepts since it focuses on scientific results rather than theoretical causal hypotheses and emphasizes accurate assessment of individual characteristics, improvement and recovery methods. For efficacy in the therapeutic arena, CT does not depend on the validity of insights into the nature of psychopathology In the assessment of treatment effects, cognitive theory first and foremost emphasizes reliable observation and measurement. Thus, cognitive theory offers a platform from which one could begin to integrate change principles and strategic definition that includes, but is not limited by, an already known array of technical interventions. Hollon and Beck (2004), for example, discuss expanding cognitive-behavioral therapy (CBT) to include elements of psychodynamic and experiential therapy. The Casebook of Psychotherapy Incorporation (2006) by Stricker and Gold offers various examples of convergence of cognitive-behavioral interventions and multiple methods of psychotherapy. Beitman, Soth, and Good (2006) describe a three-tier psycho-social therapy with assimilative (first-tier) psychodynamic therapy that combines cognitive (second-tier) and behavioral (third-tier) interventions. Ryle and McCutcheon (2006) describe cognitive analytical therapy that incorporates psychoanalytic, cognitive, constructivist, behavioral, and Vygotskian sources. McCullough (2000) describes a cognitive-behavioral psychotherapy treatment framework that incorporates Bandura's (1977) theory of social thinking, Piaget's conceptualization of cognitive-emotive development (1954/1981), interpersonal procedures à la Kiesler (1996) and situational analysis, which is a problem-solving approach to real-life circumstances.

The Range of Effectiveness Associated with Cognitive Therapy

Comparative outcome psychotherapy studies for different psychological problems have generally led to the conclusion that treatments are broadly equivalent in efficacy. Unlike those who maintain that research reveals equivalent outcomes among therapies, however, CT disciples have asserted that their treatment is more effective than others across a variety of conditions and disorders.

Studies have shown that CT is effective in treating depression of various types, such as unipolar, major, minor, and acute depression. Positive findings have also been obtained in samples of endogenous depression patients, a subtype which is often thought to be psychotherapy refractory. CT appears to be effective in reducing depression and anxiety symptoms, and in increasing assertiveness in group and individual formats. A study by Ogles, Sawyer, and Lambert (1995) for the National Institute of Mental Health found that a significant number of clients who completed cognitive depression treatment showed reliable change to all outcome measures. Brown and Barlow (1995) have observed that CT greatly decreased somatic depressive symptoms, and depressed and nervous mood among alcohol users. In addition to these studies, Scogin et al . (1987) found that cognitive bibliotherapy reduced depression more effectively than either a control group with delayed treatment or a condition with attention—placebo – bibliotherapy. While this latter observation has not been reliably confirmed, even research that fail to reproduce these results indicate that patients that score fairly high on measurements of cognitive disability appear to have lower scores on assessments of severity of depression post-treatment compared to those with higher cognitive impairment. These findings strongly imply cognitive functions as important aspects of the improvement-related change processes, regardless of the treatment model used to address them.

CT also does well in pharmacotherapy comparisons. Most published trials found that CT is at least equal to, and sometimes superior to, pharmacotherapy (Blackburn, Jones, & Lewin, 1986, 1996). In particular, studies have revealed that CT is equally or more effective than standard antidepressant drugs (Beck & Emery, 1985) and tends to have lower relapse rates (Hollon, 1996). Rush (1982), Rush, Beck, Kovacs, and Hollon (1977), Rush, Beck, Kovacs, Weissenburger, & Hollon (1982), and Murphy, Simons, Wetzel, and Lustman (1984) also discovered that CT was associated with more improvement than pharmacotherapy, and less attrition. In fact , patients were experiencing a higher dropout rate when researchers compared pharmacotherapy alone to CT. These studies also revealed that in improving depressive symptoms of hopelessness and low self-concept, CT exceeded pharmacotherapy. Even when CT is combined with pharmacotherapy, at discharge, patients tend to report significantly fewer depressive symptoms and negative cognitions than they do with pharmacotherapy alone (Bowers, 1990). CT appears to have a significant impact on the cognitive and vegetative symptoms of moderate and severe depression, as well as on the symptoms of mild and transitory depressive states.

In addition, CT has been found to be more effective than behavioral and interpersonal therapies. Gaffan, Tsaousis, and Kemp — Wheeler (1995) replicated a Dobson (1989) study which compared CT with other types of care. Although their study focused primarily on the effects of allegiance, CT was also reported to be superior to other forms of treatment, including behavioral therapy.

Clients who endorsed depression for both characterological and existential reasons responded better to CT than to behavioral interventions. Overall, there is strong support for the value of CT in treating depressed patients, but researchers are still uncertain as to the mechanisms by which this effect occurs.

CT also seems effective in the treatment of other types of disorders. CT is therefore effective in the treatment of anxiety disorders, particularly specific anxieties and phobias, and a host of other anxiety disorders and symptoms. Barlow, O'Brien, and Last (1984) and Lent, Russell, and Zamostry (1981) found CT preferable to behavioral treatment in treating depressed patients. CT also promotes total abstinence among patients with alcoholism, both at the end of the treatment and during follow-up periods. Studies further suggest that CBT is effective in treating patients with eating disorders. In patients with bulimia nervosa, Fairburn, Jones, Paveler, Hope, and O'Connor (1993) used CT and observed significant and well-maintained therapeutic outcomes mirrored in all facets of functioning. In addition, Arntz and van den Hout (1996) found that CT achieved better effects in patients with panic disorder and a secondary diagnosis of either social or mood disorder compared with mediated relaxation by reducing the incidence of panic attacks. Furthermore, CT is useful in treating patients with problems marked by a lack of self-affirmation, rage, hostility, and addiction disorders.

In addition to research investigating the impact of CT on a range of patient issues and behaviors, a rising number of literature reports have attested to the potential of CT approaches to contribute to continuous symptom reduction. For example, a 1-year follow-up analysis by Kovacs et al. (1981) showed that self-rated depression for those who had undergone CT was dramatically lower than for those diagnosed with pharmacotherapy. Similarly, a 2-year follow-up analysis of patients diagnosed with CT, pharmacotherapy or a combination reported reduced relapse levels associated with CT. In addition, patients in the pharmacotherapy group had the highest rate of relapse following 2 years. Thus, although it is uncertain what characteristics of CT yield change in various classes of patients, it is evident that CT is successful, even more efficient than other types of care.

By virtue of the variety of conditions for which it is effective, CT has certain advantages over many other models, and in that sense has the making of a flexible and eclectic intervention model. However, this does not mean the CT practice is equally effective for all individuals. Research (e.g., Beutler, Mohr, Grawe, Engle, & MacDonald, 1991) reveals that CT 's efficacy is differently influenced by a variety of patient- and problem-specific qualities. Qualities such as patient coping styles, reaction levels, and problem complexity and severity, among others, may affect the way CT is applied. One characteristic of the patient that has proven to predict the response of patients to CT is "coping style," the method that an individual adopts when confronted with anxiety-provoking situations, and that is typically seen as a trait-like pattern. CT was found to be most effective among patients exhibiting an extroverted, under-controlled, outsourcing style of coping. For example, Kadden, Cooney, and Getter (1989) evaluated alcohol patients and implemented cognitive-based social skills training as a procedure for preventing relapse through remediation of behavioral deficits in coping with interpersonal and intrapersonal drinking antecedents. Although CT was essentially as effective as other overall therapies, it was more effective than other interventions in patients that were fairly high on sociopathy or impulsivity tests. Beutler, Engle, et al . (1991) found this type of ATI, too. Depressed patients who ranked high on the Minnesota Multiphasic Personality Index (MMPI) outsourcing and impulsiveness tests reacted better to CT than to insight-oriented counseling. This pattern holds depressed patients as well as outpatients alike. Barber and Muenz (1996) have considered CT to be more effective than recovery approaches for people who escape their issues by outsourcing the blame. In addition, Beutler, Mohr, et al . (1991) and Beutler, Engle, et al . (1991) found that CT had significantly stronger effects on patients with outsourcing coping styles compared to customer-centered therapy or self-directed, supportive therapy. On the other hand, with customer-centered and self-directed therapy, internalizing patients did better than with CT. Similarly, the patient resistance traits and tendencies in the aforementioned studies differentiated the level of benefit achieved from the therapist-guided CT procedures and various patient-led or non-directive procedures.

Making Cognitive Therapy Systematically Fit Human Complexity

The main impetus for integration with psychotherapy comes from the evidence that no single psychotherapy school has demonstrated consistent superiority over the others. Instead, psychotherapy work on particular problems such as substance addiction or depression has largely contributed to the assumption that both methods have comparable average results (e.g., Lambert, Shapiro, & Bergin, 1986; Beutler, Crago, & Arizmendi, 1986; Smith, Glass, & Miller, 1980). Unfortunately, the non-significance of the main effects of treatment often draws more attention than the growing research body that shows significant differences in the types of patients for whom different aspects of treatment are effective.

Research, for example, shows that for patients with anxiety and depression symptoms:

(1) Experiential interventions are more successful than cognitive and behavioral therapy where there is inadequate initial anxiety regarding one's situation to encourage movement;

(2) Non-directive and paradoxical interventions in patients with high levels of pre-therapy resistance are more effective than guideline treatments;

(3) Interventions that address cognitive and behavioral improvements by risk management (e.g., Higgins, Budney, & Bickel, 1994) are more successful than insight-oriented therapy in impulsive or externalizing patients, but this result is reversed in patients with fewer externalizing coping types. CT should be customized to suit the complex needs and preferences of people with a wide variety of conditions and diagnoses. In a recent study at our University of California Psychotherapy Research Lab, Santa Barbara, a number of guiding principles and strategies have informed the systematic application of tactics and techniques drawn from numerous theoretical perspectives. CT techniques can be used with virtually any patient; however, the greatest benefit is achieved with differential use of strategies or techniques, depending on patient dimensions such as coping style, type of problem, subjective distress, functional and social impairment, and resistance level.

For illustrative purposes, the rest of this section addresses some of the techniques and strategies that guide the application of CT techniques to internalize or outsource the patient, the resistant patient, and to manage the level of excitement. A detailed review of the aspects of patient – care matching (resistance/reaction level, coping methods, the extent of subjective pain, and functional impairment) and guiding principles, tactics, and collection of techniques can be found elsewhere.

Patient resistance typically bodes poorly for effective treatment unless it is skillfully managed. It is generally assumed that some patients are more likely to withstand therapeutic procedures than others. "Resistance" can be characterized as a dispositional trait and a temporary in — therapy state of oppositional behaviors (e.g., angry, irritable, and suspicious). It includes both intra-psychic (picture of self, health, and psychological integrity) and interpersonal factors (loss of interpersonal control or power enforced by another). "Reactance," an extreme example of resistance, is manifested by behaviors of opposition and uncooperative.

Three hypothesized factors determine the level of resistance or reactance potential of a patient. The first element concerns the patient's intrinsic appreciation in the individual right that is considered to be in peril. For example, one patient can appreciate the freedom associated with an unfixed schedule of time commitments, while another can be relatively comfortable with a schedule or routine imposed. The second element refers to the presumed proportion of rights that are challenged or lost. The addition of a therapy item that excludes or restricts a number of freedoms (e.g., a homework task that forbids drug use and involves social contact at an event for a certain amount of time) is likely to cause a high degree of reaction among resistance-prone, alcohol-abusing, and socially disconnected individuals. The third element concerns the degree of authority and control ascribed to the person or threatening force. The resistance generated by this factor comes from the preconceived notions of a patient and the differential allocation of authority to different professional occupations (clinicians, law enforcement officers, etc.). In comparison, direct encounters with a mental health provider can be beneficial in reducing or exaggerating such conceptions.

Resistance is readily recognizable, and differentiated recovery programs are conveniently designed for people with high and low resistance. However, the successful implementation of those plans is often quite another matter. It is difficult to surmount patient resistance to the efforts of the clinician. It requires the therapist to set aside his or her own resistance in recognizing that the oppositional behavior of the patient may infact, be iatrogenic. In a study in the Vanderbilt Study of Psychodynamic Psycho-therapy of experienced and highly trained therapists, none were able to work effectively with patient resistance. Instead, therapists often responded to patient resistance by becoming angry, critical, and rejecting, which are reactions that tend to diminish patient willingness to explore problems.

In general, therapists should avoid open discord with patients who are highly resistant. CT 's collaborative relationship is an important antidote to resistance, and from the initiation of therapy this component should be emphasised.

Another common feature of CT, socratic interrogation or directed exploration, must be treated carefully to mitigate tendencies of resistance. A clinician should introduce this technique as a collaborative effort and generate feedback about the willingness of the patient to take part. The patient can also be elicited satisfaction with guidance and recommendations for exploration. Information about the level of resistance capacity of a patient can be learned from the history and actions of the patient during previous traumatic encounters or during the recovery process itself.

Research suggests that procedures that are non-directive, paradoxical, and self-directed produce better outcomes among patients with high resistance behaviors. Behavioral contracts created by patients and "suggested" homework assignments are non-directive strategies to help control resistant patients. For patients with extreme and persistent resistance, a "paradoxical intervention" might be considered in which the symptom is prescribed, or in which the patient is encouraged for a period of time to avoid change.

To put it simply, paradoxical interventions by discouraging it induce change (Seltzer, 1986). A paradoxical, non-directive intervention could involve the suggestion that the patient continue or exaggerate the symptom/behavior. A classic example of such an intervention could be the prescription of wakefulness for the insomnia complaining patient. An acceptable rationale for this type of intervention should be provided (e.g., "Your circadian rhythm is not set correctly. Staying awake will help reset your sleep cycle"). Non- or low-resistant habits suggest that patients are usually open to the therapist's external input or advice.

CHAPTER TEN

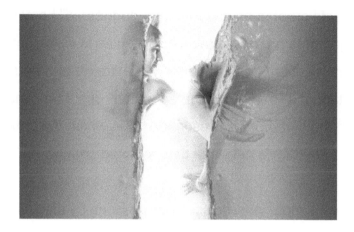

Overcoming Panic Attacks with CBT

The day-to-day tension and life's stresses can get very stressful. A lot of minor details tend to add up and ultimately lead to worry, anxiety, panic and even depression. It is only natural that the thoughts start to develop into a negative pattern from this point on. Changing the way of thinking, though, will help avoid such uncomfortable feelings. Here's some more information about cognitive behavioral therapy, which is considered by many to be the best panic attack treatment.

What Is Behavioral Cognitive Therapy?

The principle of cognitive behavioral therapy, or CBT, is that what people think will affect how they feel and behave emotionally. When under emotional distress, the manner in which someone sees and judges itself may become more negative. Therefore, CBT's aim is to help you begin to see the link between negative styles of thinking and mood. That will help you to regulate these thoughts more.

How It's Done

Cognitive behavioral therapy can be attributed to the best treatment for panic attacks, because it encourages you to develop positive thinking patterns. This happens in 3 steps: Identifying Negative Thoughts-Situations with panic disorders are perceived to be more dangerous than they actually are. Shaking another person's hand, for example, may seem like life-threatening someone with a germ phobia. Though you may think this fear is irrational, it can be very difficult to identify your own irrational, fearful thoughts. One way to do that is to remind yourself what you felt before you began feeling nervous.

Challenging Negative Thoughts-The next step is to evaluate your thought-provoking fear. Here, you'll find out how realistic your concerns are. Ask yourself whether these thoughts are true, or an exaggeration. Weigh the pros and cons of thinking and the thing you 're scared of, and assess the likelihood that it will really happen.

Replacing Negative Thoughts-You should replace them with new thoughts, which are more rational and constructive, after you have recognized the bad ideas. Instead of saying you can't do anything to yourself, tell yourself you can. Whatever happens, tell yourself you 're going to be fine. Repeat reassuring and sedative statements until you feel calm. The more confident you hear, the happier you'll be.

There are two panic attack treatments-medication, and psychological therapy. Some people advocate the former while others advocate the former; some insist on a mix of the two. It's all getting a bit confusing so how do you know which course of treatment to follow?

Firstly, when it comes to panic attacks and anxiety problems, there is no particular solution that suits all. A cornerstone of effective therapy is that after a detailed study of the symptoms and when they occur, it is tailored individually to the person. This should apply irrespective of which panic attack treatment you choose to follow-and ultimately, it is your choice and you need to feel comfortable with that.

One of the most common approaches to psychology is that of cognitive behaviour therapy or CBT. Studies have shown that CBT is much more effective than medicine in the long run. To be more precise, six months after care ended, more patients who were diagnosed with CBT were panic-free than those on the drug. Another study showed that while medication might be effective in treating panic attack symptoms, the benefits stopped when the medication stopped. That is, people were forced to continue taking the drugs which then led to unpleasant side effects.

CBT therapy requires the therapist and, more importantly, the person seeking treatment to do the work and the commitment. It's not as easy as taking drugs a couple of times a day and the effects aren't seen so quickly, but if you compare a drug-free life free from panic attacks to taking medication for the rest of your life, then the benefits are obvious.

CBT 's focus is to get you to solve the problem yourself, so that you feel in control of your life again. This is very important as one of those suffering from panic attacks' biggest fears is that they have lost control of themselves, often to the extent that they feel they are losing their minds. The 'cognitive' part of therapy means to change the way you think through a very gradual process of desensitization.

Let's say, for example, that your first attack happened in a crowded room, perhaps at a party. Because the feelings were so intense and you were so scared you would never want to experience them again. So, you 're going out of your way to avoid that situation-you 're making excuses so you don't face a recurrence. But that means you stay by yourself at home while everyone else is having fun at the dance. Not an ideal situation.

So, desensitization involves first making very small steps to get you used to the thought of going to a party (cognition) and then getting you there (behaviour). Your first step may be as if you were going to get dressed. This is it. Just dealing with the feeling you are going to be one day is enough. This can last for several days until you feel comfortable thinking you 're going to a party. You take the next move, when you're ready, which might get dressed and then open the front door as if you're on your way out. That's it for step two. The third step when you are ready is getting dressed, opening and closing the front door. And so forth.

As you go through these steps at your own pace, you will also be taught how to deal with the conflicting feelings that you have. Instrumental here is controlling your breathing. Rapid breathing is often the catalyst for the other symptoms you experience during a panic attack so if you have techniques to keep your breathing rate stable then this could be the difference between a slight twinge of anxiety and a full-blown attack.

Many therapists agree that 10-12 sessions are enough for the majority of people to be able to manage their problems alone. Upgrades can be seen after the first five or six, and the person begins to feel confident they can regain control of their lives. A final step in the recovery process is to incorporate coping strategies in the event of potential stress trying to rear its ugly head. Armed with this knowledge, the possibility of panic attacks being a thing of the past is a very real one.

CONCLUSION

There are a number of options available for those looking for methods of overcoming the anxiety that can be considered "natural." What do those natural methods of relieving anxiety involve? These are basically anti-anxiety techniques and do not require the use of prescription medications or narcotics as a way to relieve the problem. These methods often prove far more healthy than what the overused anxiety treatment methods deliver. The cognitive behavioral therapy is one such method of overcoming anxiety.

Cognitive behavioral therapy isn't new. It has been used for decades by mental health professionals as a means of altering a person's behavioral choices that create mental health problems. In addition to being used as a way of reducing fear, cognitive behavioral therapy has also been used to treat many extremely severe mental health conditions. What does cognitive therapy involve, then? Here's a short outline of what's involved:

Cognitive behavioral therapy as a form of anxiety relief involves taking a two-pronged approach to the problem. The first half includes solving the neurological problems that cause fear. That is, they will examine the thoughts and psychological components of the problem. Basically, it will examine the mental triggers that cause anxiety, and then take steps to reverse the trigger effect.

The other side of the coin is the behavior therapy component for overcoming anxiety. This approach addresses the actual triggers associated with physical actions or activities which may cause an anxiety-based reaction. As with the cognitive therapy mental component, the aim of behavioral therapy is to modify one's trigger reaction to anxiety-causing activities. Some will have legitimate questions regarding whether or not this form of treatment will lead to significant outcomes when it comes to managing anxiety. There's actually nothing to think about, as cognitive behavioural therapy has long been known to be a successful form of treatment. This is definitely not a new treatment methodology as it has been employed for many years to great success by psychologists and other mental health professionals.

One of the main reasons why cognitive behavioral therapy works as a means to enhance one's ability to gain much needed anxiety relief centers on the fact that most people don't know what causes their anxiety. In a stunning number of instances, the person experiencing the problem is completely unknown to the triggers that cause the onset of anxiety , stress, or a panic attack. The ability to get to the core of what creates the anxiety is made possible through working with a therapist. From this, it becomes possible to overcome anxiety because it identifies the root of the problem.

It's an almost difficult challenge to conquer fear by going to the root of raising the tension of your life. Naturally, if you want to experience relief from anxiety, you will need to take control of all the things that cause you stress and anxiety in your life.

Lightning Source UK Ltd.
Milton Keynes UK
UKHW021833010321
379622UK00003B/581